POWER AND PARTY BUREAUCRACY IN BRITAIN

Power and Party Bureaucracy in Britain

Regional organisation in the Conservative and Labour parties

DAVID J. WILSON
Senior Lecturer in Politics,
Leicester Polytechnic

SAXON HOUSE | LEXINGTON BOOKS

Published by

SAXON HOUSE, D. C. Heath Ltd.
Westmead, Farnborough, Hants, England.

Jointly with

LEXINGTON BOOKS, D. C. Heath & Co.
Lexington, Mass. USA

ISBN 0 347 01078 4

Printed in Great Britain by Robert MacLehose and Company Limited
Printers to the University of Glasgow

Contents

Foreword

Over the past thirty years, the study of British politics has been transformed. In the 1940s, a few formal institutional works were all that was available to the student wanting to understand the system. The political realities of parties and of pressure groups, of constituency activities and of Whitehall dealings were almost unrecorded (except between the lines of a few biographies).

Today, the facts and procedures of the power struggle at Westminster and in the country as a whole are much better known. Articles and monographs have dealt with hitherto undocumented topics ranging from candidate selection to cabinet committees and from the efficacy of canvassing to the ideology of civil servants.

But although today's student who wants to read about British government is far better off than was his father, he is still likely to be frustrated by the lack of information about how many of its institutions operate. In this book David Wilson has tackled an area which previous writers on parties have left resolutely alone.

The national parties communicate with constituency parties largely through their regional offices. When there are local rows, it is usually the area organisation that is expected to sort matters out. When candidates are chosen, it is left to the area agent to attend and to certify that there has been fair play. When a quick check on local feeling is required, it is the regional officials who are asked to phone round and report back to Smith Square.

But, until David Wilson wrote this book, no one had systematically studied the working of this essential link in British party structure. And no one had explored the dilemmas of area officials as, with no formal authority over the constituency organisations, they seek to co-ordinate party activity. The understanding of politics and elections is handicapped by the persistent use of the metaphors of war — headquarters, campaign, line of command. It is plain from this book that area agents are nothing like divisional commanders in a trained army: their main function is to make suggestions and to persuade.

It is not a very glamorous role but it is important, and David Wilson has produced what is likely to stand as the definitive work on the subject. Since documentation is limited, he has achieved this in the only way possible, by assiduous fieldwork, talking easily and frequently with the men in the field about their jobs. It is plain that he has won trust and confidence on all sides. What he sets down here has a ring of authenticity.

What is more, it challenges clichés about party structure that are too readily accepted, even by those actually involved. There is nothing very remarkable about the role of regional party organisation but, if it is misunderstood, the whole party system is misunderstood. In the past, lack of information has provided an excuse for confusion. David Wilson has now removed that excuse.

David Butler
Nuffield College,
Oxford.

Acknowledgements

This book would not have been possible without the very generous help of regional and area staff in the Labour and Conservative Parties. In addition, headquarters' staff on both sides of Smith Square have been very helpful and have encouraged me in my research. At the constituency and city party level, local party agents have spent many hours answering questions about their work. Grateful thanks are owed to them all.

I am also grateful to J.G. Bulpitt of the Department of Politics, University of Warwick, for his constructive criticism and continued encouragement while preparing for a PhD in that Department. Some of the material in this book appears in a longer work, *Regional Organisation in the Conservative and Labour Parties,* for which I was awarded a PhD in 1974. Professor Malcolm Anderson and Dr David Butler have provided some useful advice regarding publication and David Butler has also very kindly written a foreword to the book. Mrs Dorothy Bryan has typed the manuscript with great care and much patience.

Preparing a book for publication is a demanding pursuit. Throughout the long hard months my wife, Sue, showed great understanding. She not only created conditions under which I could write but she also corrected the grammar and made a great many stylistic improvements to the text. In a very real way this is as much her book as mine.

David J. Wilson
Leicester,
January 1975

Introduction

British political parties: a note on the literature

In 1967, L.D. Epstein observed: 'Writing about political parties in Western democracies is not a novel enterprise. It is several decades since political scientists, once preoccupied with constitutional forms, ceased to neglect parties.'[1]

Despite the increased interest in political parties, most British research has concentrated on either *national* or *local* organisation. Basic information about the *intermediate* level, the Labour Party's regional organisation and the Conservative Party's area structure, is not readily available. Robert McKenzie acknowledged in his own study of British parties that his prime concern was with 'the distribution of power in the Conservative and Labour Parties at the *national* level; the regional and local organisations of the two parties are, therefore, dealt with more briefly.'[2] Jean Blondel has also written: 'The eleven regions of the Labour Party and the twelve areas of the Conservative Party are rarely examined.'[3] This book sets out to fill the gap.

The literature on British political parties may be classified into three groups. Inevitably, any classification is rather arbitrary and the three selected categories are certainly not mutually exclusive. The first category consists of historical material on parties. Indeed, most studies of British political parties have been descriptive historical analyses of the origins and development of parties or, alternatively, of significant periods in their history. Secondly, a major sector of the literature has focused upon the internal power structures of the Labour and Conservative Parties. The third category delineated in this classification consists of the rapidly expanding literature on local parties.

The work at the turn of the century by M. Ostrogorski[4] and A.L. Lowell[5] provides some useful historical perspectives on the nature of nineteenth-century party organisation. They produced detailed accounts of the development of party organisation and changes in the party system caused by the extension of the franchise. Ostrogorski was particularly concerned with the caucus in England which he felt was basically undemocratic, leading to corruption and oligarchy. Recent research by J. Cornford,[6] E. Feuchtwanger[7] and R. Blake[8] has further elaborated the

1

development of Conservative party organisation. A major study by J.R. Vincent on the formation of the Liberal Party includes sections on this topic.[9] On the Labour side, important contributions to the analysis of early party organisation have been made by G.D.H. Cole,[10] H. Pelling[11] and F. Bealey. [12]

In the second category, a major study by R.T. McKenzie has examined in detail the distribution of power in the Labour and Conservative Parties. He concluded that, despite their very different origins, traditions and formal structures, power in both parties is concentrated in the parliamentary parties, particularly in the respective leaderships.[13] McKenzie followed many of the hypotheses established by R. Michels in his book *Political Parties,* published in 1915. Michels set out to demonstrate that the advent of democracy was impossible in all large organisations. Basing his research primarily on the German Social Democratic Party, he revealed the oligarchical, undemocratic nature of party organisation. Martin Harrison's study, *Trade Unions and the Labour Party since 1945,* analyses the role of the trade union movement within the Labour Party's power structure.[14] Valuable information about party organisation can be found in the Nuffield General Election studies. For example, the analysis of the 1970 General Election by David Butler and Michael Pinto-Duschinsky contains a detailed discussion of party activity at both national and local level.[15] Research on the selection of parliamentary candidates has also provided some useful insights into the nature of constituency organisation.[16] An excellent study by Richard Rose, *The Problem of Party Government,*[17] contains some detailed material about party organisation in Britain.

Much recent research into political parties has focused on particular aspects of local politics. A great deal of material on constituency parties, candidate selection and local party bureaucrats has emanated from this third category. In 1959, A.H. Birch edited a study of politics in Glossop that included an examination of the political parties in the town. [18] Some years later, Frank Bealey published a study of local politics in Newcastle-under-Lyme that provided some interesting perspectives on a local political system. [19] Two studies of borough politics produced in the 1960s have also been particularly informative, namely, *Voting in Cities: The 1964 Borough Elections* [20] and *Borough Politics.* [21] Further studies of local politics have been written by E.G. Janosik [22] and Ian Budge. [23] There are useful accounts of constituency electioneering in recent studies by Holt and Turner [24] and by Denis Kavanagh. [25] Two brief studies of local party agents by G.O. Comfort [26] and A. Fawcett [27] provide information on constituency party organisation. Somewhat later, in 1970, an important study on the size and composition of local party

2

membership was published [28] and an interesting, if heavily criticised, study of the Liverpool Labour Party appeared the following year. [29]

This discussion of the literature on British political parties has been extremely selective, focusing on the work most relevant to this study of party organisation. The most comprehensive analyses of the Labour and Conservative Parties have been made by R.T. McKenzie [30] and Richard Rose,[31] but our knowledge of British parties still contains many gaps that need to be filled. One such gap is the intermediate level in each party, the Labour Party's regional organisation and the Conservative Party's area organisation.

The framework of analysis

This study shows both the Conservative and Labour Parties as exemplifying some of the complexities of power and influence evident in any large organisation which is part bureaucracy and part a voluntary association. The particular focus of this book is the intermediate level of organisation in each party. The work of the regional bureaucrats in the two parties is examined in detail along with their organisational relationships with national, constituency and city units. In analysing the work of regional organisers and area agents, the book challenges traditional academic wisdom concerning the level of centralisation in the Labour and Conservative Parties. [32]

Both the Labour and Conservative Parties have established networks of regional offices in Britain. In 1974, the Labour Party had twelve regional offices in England, Scotland and Wales, while the Conservative Party had twelve area offices in England and Wales as well as a separate Scottish organisation. (See page 10.) Regional and area bureaucrats operate at an intermediate level, between the national party machine on the one hand and constituency associations on the other. They are employed by the centre and act as the 'eyes and ears' or the 'listening posts' of their respective leaderships, providing detailed information on constituency and local party matters for headquarters. They are also involved in servicing constituency and local parties, a task which assumes particular importance when a local unit is both politically marginal and poorly organised. In short, regional organisers and area agents exist to serve others: either the national party machine or constituency parties. A central proposition of this book is that both regional organisers and area agents act as the field administrative agents of their respective head offices. The relationship between the head office and regional bureaucrats may be described as centralised. Most important organisational initiatives are taken nationally, and regional organisers and area agents work under the close supervision of the centre.

The major reason for the development and maintenance of a field administrative network in both parties appears to be administrative convenience. The centralised relationship existing between the head offices and their regional staff is very much in line with traditional thinking about British political parties. This theme of centralised parties with powerful leaderships and relatively weak local party units has been prominent in most studies from the turn of the century onwards. According to Ostrogorski:

> ... without even resorting to much wire-pulling, the [Conservative] Central Office ensures the organisation of the party a complete unity of management which makes all the threads converge in the London office. ... Possessing the reality of power, the organisation of the leaders looks on that of the popular [National] Union as harmless and as even serving the purpose of a safety valve to let off the gas. [33]

Lowell's view, a few years later, was very similar:

> Both the Conservative and Liberal organisations are shams, but with this difference, that the Conservative organisation is a transparent, and the Liberal an opaque, sham. [34]

In 1930, J.K. Pollock wrote:

> Political organisation in Britain has become more mechanical, more controlled from the centre ... the leader of the party holds the power. ... The organisation is his tool and it responds to his deliberations. [35]

In his study of British parties, R.T. McKenzie observed that:

> Central Office is in effect the 'personal machine' of the Leader. ... *It would be difficult to envisage a more tight-knit system of oligarchical control of the affairs of a political party.* ... The party bureaucracy, responsible only to the leader of the Party, is just as fully in control of the affairs of the Party as it was in the heyday of Captain Middleton sixty years ago. [36]

Again, to quote McKenzie:

> No emphasis on the auxiliary functions of the mass organisations outside Parliament can be allowed to obscure the basic proposition

that the mass parties are primarily the servants of their respective parliamentary parties; that their principal function is to sustain teams of parliamentary leaders between whom the electorate is periodically invited to choose. [37]

Austin Ranney has put forward a similar interpretation:

> British constituency parties are not local in the same sense as American State and local parties. They are manned by activists primarily loyal to the national parties' leaders and causes. Each is established for an essentially national purpose, to elect a Member of Parliament. Everything else is subordinate to that purpose. [38]

Almost without exception, commentaries on British politics have stressed the strength of the respective party leaderships. The major function of local parties is seen to be one of acting as electoral agents for the national party machines. This widely held viewpoint tends to exaggerate the degree of centralisation inherent in both the Labour and Conservative Parties. It is argued in this study that, while regional organisers and area agents enjoy a centralised relationship with their respective head offices, constituency parties are not obliged to follow directives issued by regional or area staff. There are, however, some exceptions to this general rule, notably in the Labour Party, that will be outlined later in the book.

The deeply-rooted theme of centralisation, implicit in most studies of British parties, is not unambiguous. The term 'centralisation' itself poses many problems of analysis. As de Tocqueville wrote in his classic, *Democracy in America:* 'Centralisation is a word in general and daily use, without any precise meaning being attached to it.'[39] When the issue is discussed by political scientists, the virtues of decentralisation and the drawbacks of centralisation are almost always emphasised. A.H. Hanson has observed: 'The word decentralisation usually produces favourable reactions. Centralisation is associated with delay, red tape, and the erosion of local liberties; decentralisation with speed, initiative and grass roots participation in the decision-making process.'[40] Because the subject has often been dealt with emotionally rather than scientifically,[41] the term centralisation has acquired rather sinister connotations. Nevertheless, many of the prejudices against centralised political systems are without foundation as, for example, J.G. Bulpitt and J.W. Fesler have indicated. [42]

Fesler argues that centralisation and decentralisation are best regarded as opposite tendencies on a single continuum whose poles are beyond the range of any real political system. Total decentralisation would, according

5

to Fesler, require the state to wither away, whereas total centralisation would imperil the state's capacity to perform its functions. Given such a continuum, it is then argued that it is possible to compare political or administrative systems. Again, Fesler suggests that it should also be possible to characterise any single system over a given time period as moving toward one or other pole. [43] This analysis is useful but it overlooks one major difficulty — namely that of measuring the degree of centralisation or decentralisation in any political system. It is relatively simple to produce generalisations but these are of limited use. In practice, central relations are often too uneven and patchy to allow meaningful generalisations. For example, central authorities may treat certain areas very differently from the rest, and J.G. Bulpitt adds that:

> . . . the traditional tools used to measure centralisation and decentralisation have an excessive legalistic bias. For example, an *ultra vires* rule, a prefectoral system, grants-in-aid topping the magic 50 per cent, the loss of important functions, these factors, even when taken together, tell only part of the story and one which can be interpreted in different ways. [44]

The terms centralisation and decentralisation therefore pose problems of analysis for political scientists, and should be used with great care. Decentralisation of workload by both Labour and Conservative Party head offices is a recurring theme in this book. It is important, however, to recognise that decentralisation of workload is not identical to the decentralisation of administrative and political power. It may be both efficient and convenient to move workload out of the capital, but it may not involve any decentralisation of either administrative or political initiative. Indeed, the desire to shed workload while retaining administrative initiative at the centre has been a general characteristic of central–local relations in Britain. The Conservative and Labour Parties both reflect this tradition.

It is argued in this study that the large degree of control exercised by the respective head offices over their regional officials does not in itself establish that the two parties are highly centralised. There is no evidence to suggest that the chain of command from the centre extends beyond the regional and area bureaucrats to constituency parties. It is suggested that regional organisers and area agents cannot act as centralising agents for their parties because, although their own relationship with the centre is tightly controlled, they themselves lack any formal authority at either constituency or local party level. However, because the concept of authority, like the related concepts of power and influence, is used in a variety of ways in political science, clarification is essential.

Since the emergence of the social sciences, *authority* has been the subject of research in a wide variety of empirical settings: the family, small groups, armies and so on. This concept is also useful in analysing the nature of political parties, and the major treatment of the concept of authority in the twentieth century was that carried out by Max Weber.[45] Weber distinguished between three pure types of authority: legal—rational, traditional, and charismatic. In the last two instances, the obligation is to a person, the traditional chief or the heroic leader. Legal authority is more restricted in scope; obedience is owed to the legally established impersonal network of positions. Weber's treatment of legal—rational authority, which distinguishes between, but does not elaborate on, authority inherent in office and authority based on technical knowledge, provides the basic framework for most contemporary analyses of bureaucracy.

Political and social scientists, however, are by no means agreed on how the concept of authority should be used. For example, Michels defines authority as 'the capacity, innate or acquired, for exercising ascendancy over a group'. [46] Bierstedt, however, takes issue with each of these points, arguing that authority is not a capacity, but a relationship, and furthermore, is neither innate, nor a matter of exercising ascendancy. Although Bierstedt considers that Michels has confused authority with competence, both agree on the close relationship between authority and power. For Michels, 'authority is a manifestation of power',[47] for Bierstedt, 'authority becomes a power phenomenon . . . it is sanctioned power, institutionalised power'.[48]

Contemporary political science is no less confused. Thus, Lasswell and Kaplan define authority as 'formal power', [49] while Friedrich explicitly rejects this notion and defines it as 'the quality of communication', which is 'capable of reasoned elaboration'. [50] They are also in disagreement as to whether 'power' or 'influence' is the more inclusive term. Lasswell and Kaplan argue that 'power is a form of influence', [51] while Friedrich maintains that 'influence is a kind of power, indirect and unstructured'.[52] It is of little value to pursue a definition of authority as a special type of power and influence since political scientists have not yet formulated a widely accepted operational definition of power.

The notion of power is frequently talked about without any precise meaning being attached to it. Traditionally, political theorists have taken it for granted that key terms like power, influence and authority need no great elaboration and their application to particular situations is rarely consistent. Perhaps the closest equivalent to the power relationship is the causal relationship. For the assertion: 'C has power over R', one can substitute: 'C's behaviour causes R's behaviour'. Provided one can define the causal relationship, one can define influence, power, or authority, and vice versa. [53] Yet this approach runs into the same difficulties that have plagued efforts to distinguish true from spurious causal relations.

Until recently, the whole approach to the analysis of power was somewhat speculative: there were a good many impressionistic works but few systematic empirical studies of power relations. While the attempt to understand political systems by analysing power relations is ancient, the systematic study of power relations is relatively new. [54] The only common factor in studies of power, influence and authority is confusion.

It is suggested in this study that regional organisers and area agents lack authority at constituency and local party levels. Authority, in this sense, means little other than formal power or institutionalised power. The close relationship between authority and power is very evident, and for Lasswell and Kaplan, 'political science, as an empirical discipline, is the study of the shaping and sharing of power'.[55] Whether or not one adopts this extreme view of the importance of power, power relations are certainly one of the many features of politics and, as such, merit examination. Perhaps, as suggested earlier, the most useful equivalent to the power relation in the context of this study is the causal relation. In the context of this analysis of party organisation, influence may be understood as an indirect and unstructured kind of power relying largely on informal rather than formal relationships.

While this book argues that the well-established notion of two highly centralised parties is in need of modification, the precise relationships between the various organisational levels are complex and prohibit the formulation of a simple analytical model. For example, the relationship of regional and area staff to their respective head offices is very different from that of regional and area staff to constituency party units. [56] The following figure provides a pictorial analysis of the relationship:

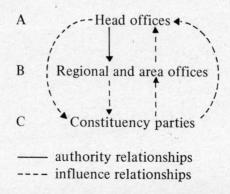

A   ---Head offices ◄- -

B   Regional and area offices

C   Constituency parties

——— authority relationships
- - - - influence relationships

The only 'authority' relationship in the model outlined above is that between the respective head offices and their regional staffs. There is no chain of command from the party leaderships to constituency and branch levels via the regional and area bureaucrats. The chain of command from the centre ends at the regional level. There are, on occasions, it is true, direct links between the centre and the constituencies (such as, for example, at annual party conferences and on national committees) but here, given the relative autonomy of constituency parties, the relationship tends to be one of two-way influence rather than that of the imposition of authority by the central party organisation. Constituency parties are voluntary associations, not always amenable to pressure from Head Office, whether or not it comes via the regional or area organiser. While the relationship of regional organisers and area agents with their respective head offices is centralised, the voluntary nature of constituency parties often makes it very difficult for regional and area organisers to exert influence, let alone authority, at the local level.

It has already been proposed that regional organisers and area agents act as the field administrative agents for their respective leaderships. The term 'field administration' is used to designate a government's or agency's administrative operations outside its national headquarters. In Europe, the term 'field administration' is usually held to be synonymous with that of 'prefect' and all the peculiar practices which were, and still are, supposed to be inherent in that office — but this is a very narrow way of looking at these agencies. Today, field administrators carry out a wide variety of tasks. According to R.C. Fried, three types of field administration can be distinguished: the *functional* and two prefectoral varieties which are differentiated according to whether or not the chief executive in the field commands a closely integrated system of decentralised administration. He terms the latter *integrated* and *unintegrated prefectoral* systems.[57]

It is suggested in this study that, in both the Labour and Conservative Parties, administrative expediency, rather than any excessive zeal for intra-party democracy, has very largely accounted for the development of regional and area units, and that this has also been an important factor in explaining their maintenance and expansion. It is difficult to categorise regional and area staff on the basis of the above models. Regional organisers and area agents are geographically based — they are generalists rather than functional specialists. At the same time, they enjoy a hierarchical relationship with their head offices, acting as the agents of the respective party leaderships and fulfilling a wide variety of tasks on their behalf. Although there are, of course, differences between the two parties which will be examined, this book argues that regional and area staff exist to serve others. On the one hand, they are employed by, and work for, the national party organisations; on the other hand, they service constituency and local parties. The relationships between the various levels in the two parties are complex and merit close examination.

Organisation of the book

In discussing the work of regional organisers and area agents this book draws largely on material from three English regions: the North-West, the West Midlands, and the East Midlands, although reference is made to other English regions as well as to Wales and Scotland. In 1974, the Conservative Party partitioned England and Wales into the following areas: Greater London North (56 constituencies), Greater London South (36), Northern (34), North-Western (78), Yorkshire (53), East Midlands (42), West Midlands (61), Eastern (45), South-Eastern (40), Wessex (42), Western (29), and Wales (36). The 71 Scottish constituencies had a separate organisational structure with their own director and deputy director of organisation. Excluding Scotland, the Conservative Party employed 12 area agents and 28 deputy area agents in 1974. In the same year, the Labour Party divided England, Scotland and Wales into the following twelve regions: Northern (37 constituencies), North-East (50), North-West (79), East Midlands (41), West Midlands (56), Eastern (45), London North (47), London South (45), South (73), South-West (43), Wales (36) and Scotland (71). At that time, there was a total of 12 regional organisers plus a general secretary and assistant secretary in Greater London. There were also 26 assistant regional organisers (two in each regional unit with a third in Scotland and the North-West). All these regional/area staff were employed by their respective head offices.

Much of the information utilised in this book had to be obtained from primary sources, notably interviews and party documents. This reliance upon primary material was inevitable, given the lack of published work. The extensive archives at most regional and area offices were particularly useful, yet this source has hitherto been largely neglected by political scientists.

Chapter 1 examines the evolution of the Conservative Party's area organisation, tracing its origins from the demands, in the late nineteenth century, by the newly enfranchised urban leaders for some recognition of their electoral importance. Chapter 2 looks at the more recent advent of the Labour Party's regional organisation, which was stimulated by the need to provide some standardisation and to equip the party for electoral politics. However, it will be argued that the major reason for the emergence, and subsequent development, of intermediate party organisation in both parties was administrative expediency.

Chapter 3 examines the relationship between regional and area organisers and their respective head offices. Regional/area reports and other documents provide the source material for this chapter, which suggests that, within the nationally determined frameworks of action, both regional organisers and area agents are afforded some initiative. Despite some differences in emphasis, the chapter argues that both parties have a similar pattern; they both employ their regional staffs to act as field agents for the respective leaderships.

A major theme of this study is the relationship between regional/area offices and constituency parties. Chapter 4 provides a detailed account of the constituency/regional relationship in action. It examines the nature and extent of work in which both regional and area staff are involved at this level. Chapter 5 follows on by providing a framework of analysis for the constituency/regional relationship. It discusses some of the most important factors determining the extent of regional and area intervention at constituency level; the authority/influence of regional and area staff at constituency level; the professionalism of local party organisation; and the financial position of constituency parties. It also examines to what extent, if at all, interference from regional and area officials poses a threat to constituency party autonomy.

City parties are sufficiently distinct from constituency associations to merit separate examination. Chapter 6 deals with the relationship between the city parties and the professional organisers at the regional and area level. Tensions between the city parties and regional/area officials often run deeper than those between regional/area offices and constituency parties. These tensions are far greater than simple personality differences; they have their origins in the rather uncertain constitutional position of the city and regional/area offices.

This book is primarily concerned with examining the role of professional party bureaucrats at the regional and area level. To carry out at least some of their duties, regional and area staff in both parties must work with the democratic structure which exists at this level. It is argued in Chapter 7 that the democratic structures at the intermediate level in both parties are certainly influenced, if not controlled, by the regional and area organisers.

General Elections are, in many respects, the organisational climax to the work carried out at the regional and area level. Chapter 8 examines regional and area activity during the 1970 and the two 1974 General

Elections. The relatively poor state of the Labour Party's constituency organisation necessitated far more detailed intervention than was needed in the Conservative Party. The usefulness of Conservative Party area staff during a General Election, however, is open to question; Labour Party regional organisers appear to be used to a far greater degree than their Conservative counterparts.

The study concludes, in Chapter 9, by providing some generalisations about the nature of regional and area party organisation in Britain. It discusses the problems of applying a single analytical model to the various regional relationships. It also outlines the major differences between the parties at the regional/area level. The importance of regional/area bureaucrats in the overall work of the Labour and Conservative Parties is also considered, along with the contribution which this study makes to contemporary political science.

Notes

[1] L.D. Epstein, *Political Parties in Western Democracies*, London 1967, p. 3.

[2] R.T. McKenzie, *British Political Parties*, Second Edition, London 1967, p. 231.

[3] J. Blondel, *Voters, Parties and Leaders*, Harmondsworth 1963, p. 108.

[4] M. Ostrogorski, *Democracy and the Organisation of Political Parties*, 2 vols, London 1902.

[5] A.L. Lowell, *The Government of England*, 2 vols, New York 1908.

[6] J. Cornford, 'The Transformation of Conservatism in the Late Nineteenth Century', *Victorian Studies*, VII, 1963, p. 41.

[7] E. Feuchtwanger, *Disraeli, Democracy and the Tory Party*, London 1968.

[8] R. Blake, *The Conservative Party from Peel to Churchill*, London 1968.

[9] J.R. Vincent, *The Formation of the British Liberal Party*, London 1966.

[10] G.D.H. Cole, *British Working Class Politics, 1832–1914*, London 1941.

[11] H. Pelling, *Origins of the Labour Party*, London 1965.

[12] F. Bealey and H. Pelling, *Labour and Politics, 1900–1906*, London 1958.

[13] R.T. McKenzie, op.cit., 1967.

[14] M. Harrison, *Trade Unions and the Labour Party since 1945*, London 1960.

[15] D. Butler and M. Pinto-Duschinsky, *The British General Election of 1970*, London 1971. See also D. Butler and D. Kavanagh, *The British General Election of February 1974*, London 1974.

[16] See, for example, A. Ranney, *Pathways to Parliament*, London 1965; M. Rush, *The Selection of Parliamentary Candidates*, London 1969; and P. Paterson, *The Selectorate*, London 1967.

[17] R. Rose, *The Problem of Party Government*, London 1974.

[18] A.H. Birch, *Small Town Politics*, London 1959.

[19] F. Bealey, et al., *Constituency Politics*, London 1965.

[20] L.J. Sharpe, *Voting in Cities: the 1964 Borough Elections*, London 1967.

[21] G.W. Jones, *Borough Politics*, London 1969.

[22] E.G. Janosik, *Constituency Labour Parties in Britain*, London 1968.

[23] I. Budge, et al., *Political Stratification and Democracy*, London 1972.

[24] R.T. Holt and J.E. Turner, *The Battle of Barons Court*, London 1968.

[25] D. Kavanagh, *Constituency Electioneering in Britain*, London 1968.

[26] G.O. Comfort, *Professional Politicians: A Study of British Party Agents*, Washington D.C. 1958.

[27] A. Fawcett, *Conservative Agent*, London 1967.

[28] D. Berry, *The Sociology of Grass Roots Politics: A Study of Party Membership*, London 1970.

[29] B. Hindess, *The Decline of Working Class Politics*, London 1971. For a penetrating critique of this book see R. Baxter, 'The Working Class and Labour Politics' in *Political Studies*, March 1972, pp. 97–107.

[30] R.T. McKenzie, op.cit.

[31] R. Rose, op.cit.

[32] The traditional wisdom concerning the degree of centralisation in the Labour and Conservative Parties is exemplified in, for example: M. Ostrogorski, op.cit; A.L. Lowell, op.cit; J.K. Pollock, 'British Party Organisation' in *Political Science Quarterly*, XLVI, 1930; R.T. McKenzie, op.cit. To date, the major critique of this view has come from Michael Pinto-Duschinsky, *The Role of Constituency Associations in the Conservative Party*, PhD Thesis, Oxford 1972, but this analysis is obviously restricted to the Conservative Party. See also Michael Pinto-Duschinsky, 'Central Office and Power in the Conservative Party', *Political Studies*, XX, March 1972.

[33] M. Ostrogorski, op.cit., pp. 526, 527.

[34] A.L. Lowell, op.cit., p. 578.

[35] J.K. Pollock, op.cit., p. 180.

[36] R.T. McKenzie, op.cit., pp. 17, 291. (McKenzie's italics.)

[37] Ibid., p. 647.

[38] A. Ranney, op.cit., p. 281.

[39] A. de Tocqueville, *Democracy in America* (Mentor Edition), New York 1956, p. 63.

[40] A.H. Hanson, 'Decentralization' in *Planning and the Politicians,* London 1969, p. 104.

[41] The major exception here is the work of J.W. Fesler. See, for example, 'Approaches to the Understanding of Decentralisation' in *The Journal of Politics,* XXVII, 1965.

[42] J.G. Bulpitt, 'Participation and Local Government: Territorial Democracy' in *Participation and Politics,* edited by G. Parry, Manchester 1972; J.W. Fesler, 'The Political Role of Field Administration' in F. Heady and S.L. Stokes, *Papers in Comparative Public Administration,* New York 1962.

[43] J.W. Fesler, 'Centralisation and Decentralisation' in *International Encyclopaedia of the Social Sciences,* New York 1968, p. 371.

[44] J.G. Bulpitt, op.cit., p. 299.

[45] M. Weber, *The Theory of Social and Economic Organisation,* London 1922.

[46] R. Michels, 'Authority', in *Encyclopaedia of the Social Sciences,* New York 1930, p. 319.

[47] Ibid., p. 319.

[48] R. Bierstedt, 'The Problem of Authority', in M. Berger, et al. (eds), *Freedom and Control in Modern Society,* New York 1954, pp. 79, 80.

[49] H.D. Lasswell and A. Kaplan, *Power and Society: A Framework for Political Inquiry,* London 1950, p. 133.

[50] C.J. Friedrich, *Man and His Government: An Empirical Theory of Politics,* New York 1963, chapters 9–13.

[51] H.D. Lasswell and A. Kaplan, op.cit., p. 85.

[52] C.J. Friedrich, op.cit., p. 199.

[53] H.A. Simon, *Models of Man,* New York 1957.

[54] See the massive literature on community power in American cities. The alternative approaches and general confusion in these studies is indicative of the confusion in the area of power relations in politics.

[55] H.D. Lasswell and A. Kaplan, op.cit., p. xiv.

[56] Constituency parties, in this context, are the official party organisations in each Parliamentary constituency. In both parties, they elect their own officers and adopt their own candidates for Parliamentary

elections. Usually each constituency party raises and administers its own funds, owns or rents its offices and conducts its own local publicity and propaganda for the party. Some constituency parties also employ a full-time agent.

57 See R.C. Fried, *The Italian Prefects,* New York 1963; J.W. Fesler, 'Field Organisation' in F.M. Marx, *Elements of Public Administration,* New Jersey 1959; B.C. Smith, *Field Administration,* London 1967.

1   The Evolution of Conservative Party Area Organisation

Nineteenth-century origins

The Conservative Party's area structure was established primarily to provide convenient administrative units through which the leadership could supervise its extra-parliamentary organisation. It is argued in this study that the evolution of Conservative Party area organisation must be seen not only in the context of the decentralisation of a national party machine, but also as one element in the democratisation of party organisation. The Conservative Party's present area structure is the product of history, and an account of its evolution is necessary in order to put the contemporary position into perspective.

This area structure dates from May 1886 when, 'at a special conference held at the Westminster Palace Hotel (now Abbey House) it was decided to promote the more efficient organisation of the National Union by forming ten provincial divisions, eight in England and two in Wales'.[1] Pressure from the party's urban leaders was a major factor accounting for the establishment of area organisation[2] but the turmoil in the party caused by Randolph Churchill's bid for power was also important.[3] The area structure was established partly as a 'safeguard against popular caprice and personal ambition. The areas were expected to act like watertight compartments, as it was believed that all ten divisions would not go mad at once, and that any man would find it very hard to capture enough of them one at a time, to control the Union.'[4] Provincial unions were, therefore, created by the Conservative Party leadership, partly because of pressure from the grass roots, but also to safeguard its own position.

Administratively, provincial unions soon proved to be very useful. They provided a convenient means for communicating party policy and also for supervising the party more effectively from headquarters. The leadership immediately showed a very clear desire to influence, if not control, these new organisational units. The Conservative Party's principal agent and one of the party whips were given *ex officio* seats on the Council and Executive Committee of each provincial union. In the Midlands area, for example, the first annual report observed that E. Ashmead-Bartlett, MP, Chairman of the National Union, R.R. Akers-Douglas, MP, Parliamentary Whip, and Captain R.W.E. Middleton, Principal Agent of the Party, were all made *ex officio* members of the provincial union's Executive Committee.[5] Far more importantly, the leadership appointed a paid agent in each area, chosen nationally and financed by central party funds. This agent also acted as secretary of his provincial union, thereby helping to ensure some supervision of each union.

The 1886 reorganisation had far-reaching implications which have been summarised as follows by Ostrogorski:

> Without possessing any formal power in them, the provincial agent of the Central Office nevertheless controls all the local associations of the Union, thanks to the fact that he represents the Central Office not only with the prestige as the organ of the great leaders, but also with its resources of which the associations so often stand in need — speakers for the meetings, political literature, and last, but not least, money; an association which does not try to conciliate the agent of the Central Office would not obtain any assistance. To this material power it adds the seduction of civility to the secretaries of the local association. Thus, without even resorting to much wire-pulling, the Central Office controls the organisation of the party, a complete unity of management which makes all the threads converge in the London office and utilizes the popular associations for its own ends, so as to get hold of the voters all the more easily.[6]

Given his scepticism of party organisation, perhaps Ostrogorski was not a good witness, but the theme of increased central supervision of local organisation does seem justified.

Central Office versus the National Union, 1900–11

Except for a period of three years, the Conservatives were continuously in power between 1886 and 1906. Party organisation was not, therefore, a major priority. During these years, there were, however, periodic protests from the grass roots concerning the degree of central control over provincial organisation. At the 1887 Annual Conference, for example, one delegate proposed that the new unions should be given the task of organising meetings and lectures in their respective districts. Central Office opposed this vigorously, arguing that such an extension of provincial union power would weaken the hands of the Central Executive.[7] Reaction against Central Office was, however, closely tied up with the factional struggles within the Conservative Party at the turn of the century. For example, following the 1906 General Election when Central Office was very much the preserve of the Balfourite wing of the party, the Chamberlainite faction outnumbered the Balfourites by 102 to 36, and the scene was set for organisational reform.

In the party reorganisation of 1906, the National Union's powers were increased (albeit temporarily) at the provincial level at the expense of Central Office. Chamberlain's animosity towards Central Office was particularly marked: 'As far as my information goes, the Central Office is as bad as ever, and in all negotiations between it and the country organisation it leans heavily against Tariff Reformers and in favour of the Free Food section.'[8] Central Office was the major centre of organisational resistance to Chamberlain and the Tariff Reformers, and, with the Balfourites remaining firmly in control at Central Office, Chamberlain and his followers were obliged to turn elsewhere in their attempts to topple the old guard, so they attempted to undercut the powers of Central Office by widening the authority of the National Union. Chamberlain was on firm ground in moving in this direction. In the party as a whole, there had been considerable dissatisfaction with Central Office for some years previously, and the 1906 defeat strengthened the hand of those members who had been calling for the party's democratisation.

Partly to appease the impatience with Central Office control, the responsibility of the National Union 'for the superintendence of organisation, the provision of literature and party speakers (other than MPs)'[9] was emphasised. At the area level, the area agents, employed by Central Office, were relieved of their secretarial duties towards the provincial councils. In future, the secretary was to be chosen and financed locally rather than by Central Office. 'Yet these changes were ill-conceived, partly because factional considerations were given more weight than organisational considerations. They emphasised the debilitating dualism of the party organisation, and impaired its electoral efficiency.'[10]

Following these reforms, Central Office agreed to pay the National Union a fixed annual grant of some £8,500 to cover office establishment, publications and lectures, to be supplemented at by-elections by additional grants at the discretion of the principal agent and the chief whip. [11] The new division of responsibilities provided the ideal excuse for inaction on the part of Central Office, particularly at the local level, and also gave rise to gross inefficiencies. Further reform, however, was imminent.

In 1911, Balfour appointed a special committee to examine party organisation, and the resultant reforms were far more drastic than those of 1906. Whereas the 1906 reforms 'had seen the transference of authority from an overburdened Central Office to a reorganised National Union. . . the changes of 1911 saw a restoration to a reformed Central Office of the authority it had formerly surrendered'.[12] In that year, following the withdrawal of Joseph Chamberlain from the political scene, it was resolved that 'all executive power as regards organisation, literature and the provision of speakers should be vested entirely in Central Office'.[13] The National Union, which in 1906 had been the hope of the 'democratic' tendency, was firmly put in its place once again.

The inter-war years: the area pattern determined

No major demands for reform occurred until after 1923 when electoral defeat, coupled with political difficulties, once again stimulated pressure for organisational change. For example, the Central Council of the National Union passed the following resolution on 12 February 1924: 'That in the opinion of this meeting, it is desirable that more democratic methods should prevail in the councils of the party, and that a reorganisation should take place both in the constituencies and in the Central Office where it is found desirable.'[14]

The Cheshire division illustrates the impact of these recommendations at the area level. At the 1924 Annual Meeting of the Cheshire Union 'a letter was read from the Principal Agent, Mr H.E. Blain, dated 26th June, 1924, with regard to proposed alterations in the Rules of the National Unionist Association dealing with the representation of Constituency Associations on the Councils of Provincial Divisions and with the Constitution of the Central Council'.[15] In effect, Central Office was requesting the amalgamation of small provincial areas. Early in 1925, the Executive Committee of the Cheshire Provincial Union issued a report on this question:

> Your committee have now considered the whole question of amalgamation in the light of this basis of representation. Having taken into consideration the strongly expressed views of the Central Office that there are too many Provincial Divisions for effective work, and that the Central Office have already amalgamated the two Provincial Divisions of Lancashire and Cheshire for the purpose of representation on the Executive Committee in London . . . your executive recommend to the Council that the amalgamation should

be proceeded with and that the Executive Committee should be authorised to carry out the necessary details in conjunction with the Lancashire representatives.[16]

Later that year, the new Lancashire and Cheshire Provincial Union was formed, although it was not until the reorganisation of 1931 that the Central Office agent for the North-West eventually became secretary of the Provincial Council. [17]

Following the Conservative Party's defeat in the 1929 General Election the Central Council set up a sub-committee 'to consider the replies to a questionnaire issued to the chairmen of constituencies in England and Wales inquiring into the reasons for the defeat of the Party at the General Election'. Another sub-committee was appointed 'to inquire into the relationship between the National Union, the Central Office and the Leader of the Party, and to report with recommendations for alteration or improvement'. [18]

The report, presented to the Central Council on 4 March 1930, contained a number of important proposals which directly affected the party's provincial organisation. The committee argued that 'while preserving full individuality to the constituency as a unit, it is to the greater activity of the Provincial Divisions that we must look in future for a revival of local interest and a more extended means of spreading our political principles'. The addendum to the report continued:

For purposes of general organisation, the Central Office has divided England and Wales into twelve Provincial Areas, each of which is overlooked by two officials known as the Central Office Area Agents. Eight Provincial Divisions already coincide with these Central Office Areas, and we are strongly of the opinion that the sooner means can be found to federate the smaller existing Provincial Divisions into the four remaining Central Office Areas, the better it will be for our general organisation, and the more easily will the rank and file in those Areas find a means of expressing their views. We are fully aware of the difficulties in the way of federation and the fear that local feeling may be swallowed up in the larger unit. This feeling can, we consider, be maintained intact by preserving, where desired, the existing County or Grouped County organisations as units for the work they now perform, and using the larger area simply for political work which is common to the whole area. This practice is already in force in some of the larger existing Provincial Divisions and generally appears to be working successfully. There, too, local feeling has to some extent been met by holding the Provincial Division meetings in turn in the larger centres of the whole Area. We consider that the Provincial Division machinery might in the future be much more fully employed. This would, we believe, directly assist the Central Organisation of the Party by relieving it of much detail which could be better settled on the spot. [19]

This last sentence is particularly important. In both the establishment and subsequent evolution of area organisation the administrative, not the democratic, element has been uppermost.

The 1930 proposals for reforming the Conservative Party's area organisation were not readily accepted. A special one-day conference of the National Union was held in London on 1 July 1930 to discuss the issue of reform. At this meeting, there was considerable opposition to the proposed changes in the party's provincial structure. Whereas much provincial council activity had previously been organised on a county basis, the 1930 changes were designed to amalgamate these small units into more viable organisational units at the area level. There were two major themes at the conference. The most obvious was parochialism, but there was also a fear that larger units at the provincial level would weaken the representation of party members. This view was expounded by a Mr McKeagh from Bath:

> What will happen is that all but local members where the area and county conferences are held and all but the leisured and monied classes will be excluded from the Conferences. It is difficult enough to get Conservative working men and Conservative working women to the meetings, but with the increased size and the increased travelling and the increased time to be occupied, it is quite certain that we shall not be able to get to area meetings in addition to the county meetings . . . control will be vested even more in the hands of the well-to-do, so let us cut out Provincial Areas and let us concentrate on the County Provincial Divisions. . . .[20]

Opposition to the proposed restructuring was so strong that the party leadership was forced to back down. R.T. McKenzie has observed that the pattern of provincial areas 'has not been basically altered since it was established in 1930'.[21] In fact, the modern structure was not established in 1930. The components of three of the proposed provincial areas failed to amalgamate at that time. These were: (1) Middlesex and Essex; (2) Kent, Surrey and Sussex; (3) Devonshire, Somerset and Cornwall. The Conservative Party's annual reports indicate that Middlesex and Essex did not finally form the Home Counties North Division until 1938. Kent,

Surrey and Sussex finally came together in the Home Counties South-East Division in 1936, while, in 1937, Devonshire, Somerset and Cornwall formed the Western Division.

The general resistance to the 1930 reforms caused delay in their implementation. The Midlands Union, for example, retained all its existing counties except Nottinghamshire, which it lost to a newly established East Midlands Provincial Area. The exclusion of Nottinghamshire caused a storm of protest. A Midlands Union Executive Committee meeting, held on 3 April 1930, and attended by Robert Topping, Principal Agent of the Conservative Party, reflected the prevailing mood of discontent. The minutes of this meeting record that Mrs C. Margaret Harper from Central Nottingham, along with Alderman L.O. Trivett and Mrs E. Littlewood, both from Rushcliffe in Nottinghamshire, spoke against the transfer. [22] However, by 1931, Central Office had obtained its desired reorganisation in the Midlands, despite local opposition. [23]

During the 1930s, therefore, the position of Central Office in the provinces, which had been somewhat uncertain since 1906, was regularised. Its position at the area level had never been drastically weakened, even by the 1906 reorganisation. A uniform pattern of administrative units was adopted throughout England and Wales, and, with the exception of a major reorganisation in London, this pattern has remained largely unaltered.

The standardisation of Central Office influence at the provincial level was an important feature of the 1930s, affecting every organisational unit. For example, this decade saw the imposition in every area of a permanent, full-time Central Office official capable of taking responsibility for the conduct and organisation of Provincial Labour Committee affairs. [24] The full effect of this can be illustrated with reference to the Yorkshire Area. In the 1920s, the Yorkshire Federation of Labour Committees, as it had been called, had met irregularly and had failed to develop a close liaison with the Yorkshire provincial structure and had generally received little encouragement or support from the provincial leadership. Following the changes proposed nationally in 1930, the area Central Office agent, Stephen Piersenné, personally met the Federation and secured their agreement 'to alter their constitution in order to bring it into line with the National Union rules and proposed rules of the Yorkshire Provincial Division'. [25]

Piersenné appears thereafter to have played a prominent part in securing the necessary changes, and, at the inaugural meeting of the new Yorkshire Labour Advisory Committee, he himself took the chair. Moreover, in his capacity as Secretary of the Yorkshire Provincial Area

Council, he secured for himself appointment as a Joint Secretary of the Area Labour Committee, a post which he, and subsequently his successor, held throughout the 1930s. The importance of this appointment was twofold. Firstly, it ensured that agendas and minutes were properly circulated and that a full record was kept of the Area Labour Committee's activities. Secondly, the active participation of the area agent in Labour Committee affairs provided the committee with a direct link with other sectors of the provincial party organisation, so that, during that decade, the Labour Committee never appears to have become as isolated within the provincial structure as had the Labour Federation in the 1920s.

It is clear from the evidence that, in the Yorkshire Area at least, the strengthening of the Labour movement at the provincial level was largely due to the efforts of the area agents in the 1930s. It was Piersenné who, for example, met the leaders of the old Federation in Yorkshire to discuss constitutional changes. It was he who made the arrangements for the inaugural meeting of the reconstituted Area Labour Committee which he himself chaired. It was he who proposed the reimbursement of Labour delegates' travelling expenses to the Area Finance and General Purposes Committee, and he also who, as we have seen, took over the joint secretaryship of the Labour Committee. The area agent, in other words, spearheaded the campaign to establish and maintain the provincial Labour Committees during the 1930s and, given the standardisation of Central Office influence at the provincial level, there is no reason to believe that area agents in other areas were any less well placed to take similar initiatives.

Reform and change: the post-war years

Following the demands for organisational reform made after the massive Conservative defeat in the 1945 General Election, changes were made very quickly at the area level. By 1947, all twelve areas had established a Trade Union Advisory Committee, serviced by nationally employed trade union organisers. Young Conservative organisers and Conservative Political Centre (CPC) organisers were also appointed to each area. Again, these officials were appointed and financed by Central Office. There were further organisational developments in the immediate post-war era. In March 1948, the Maxwell-Fyfe Committee was set up by the Executive Committee of the National Union to examine all aspects of party organisation. This committee produced what R.T. McKenzie has described as 'the most extensive review of the party organisation which has been undertaken in this century'.[26] Amongst many other important recommendations, the Committee proposed the retention of the area structure, although it recognised 'that for certain purposes the area chairman, dealing sometimes with as many as eighty constituencies, is compelled to break down the area into smaller groups'.[27] The Committee rejected the suggestion that area agents should be appointed by the area from a panel approved by the Executive Committee of the National Union. The same issue arose in the Labour Party with a similar outcome, so that, despite pressure from the grass roots, both party leaderships have retained their powers to appoint regional and area staff.

The Maxwell-Fyfe Report consolidated the position of the area structure within the party:

> We believe that the establishment of a direct chain of communication from the chairman of the Party Organisation through Area and Constituency Chairmen down to Branch Chairmen is the most effective method by which confidential information relating to organisation may be passed. We are of the opinion that the exchange of information will greatly stimulate branches, constituencies and areas to rise to the level of the best performance.[28]

Between 1948 and 1971 two further reports on party organisation examined the area structure. In 1963, Selwyn Lloyd was asked by the Party Chairman to examine 'the need for closer liaison between Members of the Party in Parliament, the National Union and the Central Office'.[29] While accepting that the Party's area organisation had, on the whole, worked well, Lloyd proposed increasing the number of areas, a recommendation which has subsequently come to nothing. The only major change in the 1960s came with the establishment of the new Greater London Council, but this reduced rather than increased the number of areas. In 1963, the old Home Counties Area amalgamated with the old London Area, producing a new Greater London Area. Subsequently, however, this exceptionally large organisational unit split into Greater London North (56 constituencies) and Greater London South (36).

The Macleod Committee was set up in December 1964 by the Party Chairman, Lord Blakenham, to look into the Young Conservative organisation. Chapter 6 of this report examined the area structure and its importance to the organisation:

> The importance of the Area Organisation has been underrated in the past. We believe that it has a key role in ensuring that decisions and initiatives taken at national level are brought to the attention of and

acted on by the constituencies. At the same time it is responsible for communicating the ideas of constituencies to the National Advisory Committee. In addition to this the Area Organisation has the job of co-ordinating the activities of constituencies within its boundaries. [30]

Macleod proposed the creation of an Area Activity Committee and the inauguration of area plans concerned with the formation of new organisations where none existed and with 'helping constituencies to help weaker neighbours'. [31] In practice, however, the Macleod Report has not made a great impact.

During the 1960s, the Conservative Party reduced its personnel at the area level. In 1968, each area lost its specialist staff, and the work previously carried out by the area publicity officers, trade union organisers and CPC (Conservative Political Centre) organisers became the province of one person, a new deputy area agent. Anthony Barber, the Party Chairman, explained the changes at the 1968 Annual Conference:

> The system of Area Press Officers, Area CPC Officers, and Area Industrial Officers, was simply not working properly. So, after consulting the officers of the respective Advisory Committees, I came to the conclusion that the only thing to do was to scrap the old system completely and, instead, to appoint nine additional Deputy Area Agents so that the CPC and the very important matter of industrial organisation would be the special responsibility of someone at the very top in each area. Relations with press, radio and television . . . are of such importance that I decided that they should be the responsibility of the Area Agent himself.[32]

These proposals meant a net reduction of two organisers per area. The 1968 Annual Report of the North-West Area observed: 'We were all shocked to hear that as a result of the Party's serious financial position a top-level decision had to be made to dispense with the services of all Area CPC Officers, Trade Union Organisers and Area Press Officers. . . .'[33] The official reaction was one of shock rather than grief. This was because the area structure, as it existed before 1968, was not very satisfactory; it encouraged empire building, with each specialised area officer out to develop his own particular sphere of activity, irrespective of the other area units. In addition, the old system produced a situation in which there were direct links between area and Central Office specialists. For example, the press officer at area office was responsible to the press officer at Central Office, and, according to the party's Director of Organisation: 'This system caused problems for the area agent and one sometimes did not know what was going on within one's own office. There tended to be a lack of co-ordination in area office.' [34]

It appears that Sir Richard Webster has understated the difficulties presented by the presence of specialists at the area office. The complexity of the relationship between the area specialists, the area agent and Central Office can be illustrated with reference to a document issued by Eric Adamson, Head of the Labour Department at Central Office in 1939–53. He wrote:

> Organisers are employed and paid for by Central Office. They are attached to the Provincial Areas and work under the guidance and discipline of the Central Office Agent. It is the Area Agent who should say in which Constituency or District the Organiser will work and make the preliminary arrangements. There is sometimes a tendency to treat the Trade Union Organiser as a servant of the Area and to lessen the tie with the Labour Department. [On occasions there is] a demand that all reports, journals etc. must be sent to the Area Agent who will forward them to the centre. The policy laid down in regard to this, is that the weekly, monthly and six monthly reports shall be sent to Central Office with a copy to the Area. In one certain case the Area Agent has sought to prevent the Conservative Councils in his area from having direct communication with the Labour Department, informing them that all letters should be to the Area Office. [35]

In September 1974, there was a total of 40 Central Office area agents and deputies operating in the 12 English and Welsh organising areas. [36] In addition, each area had a youth organiser working under the direction of the area agent. Apart from changes in London and minor adjustments elsewhere following the 1972 Local Government Act, the contemporary area structure remains much as it was at the end of the 1930s.

Notes

[1] *The Party Organisation,* Conservative and Unionist Central Office, Organisation Series, no. 1, August 1964, p. 3.

[2] See J. Cornford, 'The Transformation of Conservatism in the Late Nineteenth Century', *Victorian Studies,* VII, 1963, p. 46.

[3] See R.T. McKenzie, *British Political Parties,* London 1963, pp. 166–73.

[4] A.L. Lowell, *The Government of England,* London 1908, p. 559.

5   1886 Annual Report, Midland Provincial Union, p. 2.

6   M. Ostrogorski, *Democracy and the Organisation of Political Parties,* London 1902, pp. 526–7.

7   1887 National Union Conference Report.

8   Quoted in P. Fraser, 'Unionism and Tariff Reform: The Crisis of 1906', *The Historical Journal,* no. 2, 1962, p. 164.

9   R.T. McKenzie, op.cit., p. 184.

10   N. Blewett, *The Peers, the Parties and the People: The General Elections of 1910,* London 1972, p. 269.

11   National Union Executive Committee Minutes, 3 June 1907.

12   R.B. Jones, 'Balfour's Reform of Party Organisation', *Bulletin of the British Institute of Historical Research,* XXXVIII, May 1965, pp. 100, 101.

13   *The Times,* 26 October 1911.

14   1924 Conservative Annual Conference Report, folio 13.

15   1924 Cheshire Provincial Union, Report of Annual Meeting.

16   1925 Cheshire Divisional Union, Executive Committee Minutes, 17 January.

17   1931 Lancashire and Cheshire Provincial Council, Executive Committee Minutes.

18   1929 Conservative Annual Conference Report.

19   *Report of the Committee on Party Organisation,* 1930.

20   Special Conference Report, 1 July 1930.

21   R.T. McKenzie, op.cit., p. 232.

22   1930 Midlands Union, Executive Committee Minutes, 3 April.

23   The minutes of the General Purposes Sub-Committee of the Midlands Union, 20 February 1931, observed: 'This county [Nottinghamshire] has seceded from the Midland Union apparently against the wishes of many of its representatives.'

24   The archive material upon which this section is based was kindly loaned to me by John R. Greenwood, a colleague at Leicester Polytechnic who is researching into the Conservative Party's trade union structure.

25   Yorkshire Provincial Area Council, Finance and General Purposes Committee Minutes, 12 February 1931.

26   R.T. McKenzie, op.cit., p. 183.

27   *Final Report of the Committee on Party Organisation* (The Maxwell-Fyfe Report), London 1949, p. 3.

28   Ibid., p. 24.

29   *The Selwyn Lloyd Report,* Conservative Central Office, London 1963, p. 3.

30   *The Macleod Report,* Conservative Central Office, London 1965, p. 16.

[31] Ibid., p. 17.

[32] 1968 Conservative Annual Conference Report, p. 24.

[33] 1968 Annual Report, North-West Provincial Area, p. 12.

[34] Interview with Sir Richard Webster, Director of Organisation, 1970.

[35] Extract from a Central Office document prepared by E.S. Adamson, outlining the position of Labour Organisers within the Party, pp. 14, 15 (author's brackets, no date given).

[36] Information from Sir Richard Webster, Director of Organisation, 10 September 1974. The two Greater London organising areas, North and South, combine to elect a Greater London area council which carries out the functions of the National Union's area units. These will be explained in Chapter 7.

2   The Advent of Labour Party Regional Organisation

Twentieth-century origins

The historical development of the Labour Party's regional organisation was somewhat different. The Labour Representation Committee was not established until 1900, and, in 1906, it changed its name to the Labour Party. At the turn of the century, the Labour Party was barely embryonic, whereas the Conservative Party had long been a political force in the land. In these early years, the Labour Party's organisation was inevitably rather primitive, and since the establishment of local Labour Parties was largely the work of pioneers in the Independent Labour Party, it was relatively slow in gaining momentum. By 1906, some 76 local Labour Parties had been established and these formed the framework of what was to develop into a national political party.[1] In the General Election of that year, the LRC fought 50 constituencies, polled over 300,000 votes and returned 29 Members of Parliament, thanks to an agreement with the Liberal Party. In February 1906, at the first meeting of the LRC's Members of Parliament, a new Parliamentary party − the Labour Party − came into existence.

While party organisation continued to develop at the constituency level, the establishment of regional machinery was not a priority in these early years. When the National Executive Committee eventually began to think about developing some form of regional organisation it met opposition stronger than that faced earlier by the Conservative Party leadership. Opposition was still very much in evidence in the 1960s, when there was a fierce outcry against the National Executive Committee's attempts to control the appointment of a general secretary to the newly established Greater London Regional Council of the Labour Party. Despite occasional difficulties, however, the NEC, like the Conservative Party leadership, has succeeded in establishing a network of regional field agents throughout the country.

The NEC's first move towards a form of regional organisation came in 1914 when Mr Ben Shaw of Glasgow was appointed as its Scottish Secretary. In 1915, Shaw also became secretary of the newly established Scottish Advisory Council. This encroachment by the National Executive Committee was challenged in Scotland, and much of the criticism was directed against a clause in the Constitution of the Scottish Advisory Council which dealt with the position of the organising secretary: 'The Organising Secretary shall be paid as a permanent official appointed by and responsible to the Executive Committee of the Labour Party.'[2] One Scottish delegate at the 1914 Annual Conference maintained that 'as the Organising Secretary would be working entirely in Scotland he should be under the control of the Executive'.[3] Nothing, however, came of this Scottish protest.

The 1918 Representation of the People Act encouraged the further development of Labour Party organisation by enfranchising all male citizens over the age of 21, as well as women over 30. Consequently, the British electorate increased from 8,357,648 in 1915 to 21,392,322 in 1918.[4] The enfranchisement of women over 30 led to the appointment in 1918 of a woman officer, Dr Marion Philips, and two national women organisers to assist organisation at constituency level. By March 1919, two more national women organisers had been appointed, and they concentrated their work on specific regions, their task being to form Women's Advisory Councils for each district. By 1919, two such councils had been established – one in Lancashire and Cheshire and the other in London.[5]

The regional solution, 1920–48

In 1914, Labour Party membership stood at 1,612,147 and, by 1920, this had risen to 4,359,807. It was against the background of franchise reform and expanding party membership that the NEC set up a sub-committee to review the whole system of party organisation. On the recommendation of this sub-committee, the NEC decided that organisational improvements were necessary and proposed the division of England, Scotland and Wales into eight organising areas. The NEC's report to the 1920 Annual Conference stated:

> The present method of having two organisers travelling the whole country has served its purpose, and with the growth of the party, and the increased constituencies a more direct and comprehensive method is required. The effect of the new scheme will be to bring the whole country into personal touch with the national staff, to ensure personal visitation, consultation, inspection and report, and to bring every part of the country under the special charge of a district organiser, with the assistance of a woman organiser in each area.[6]

The new regional organisers were to be selected and employed nationally rather than locally; they were to be the agents of the NEC at regional level. The increase in affiliation fees, granted by the 1920 Annual Conference, enabled the NEC to establish this new scheme. In the event, however, the country was divided into nine rather than eight organising districts,[7] each with a district (or regional) organiser and a women's organiser. These were as follows: North-Eastern, North-Western, Midlands, Southern and Home Counties, London, South-Western, Eastern, Wales and Monmouth, Scotland.

By 1921, therefore, a network of regional organisers had been established to deal with the tremendous increase in both working class voters and party members after the First World War. The national agent was responsible for arranging and directing the work of the organisers:

> The work of the district organisers will be to act under the direction of the National Agent in inspecting, advising, and consulting with the agents in the constituencies, developing organisation in areas where divisional and local parties are not at present formed, and to assist in the training of agents in connection with the Head Office Scheme and generally to co-operate in the organisation work of the Party as required by the Head Office.[8]

Thus their position *vis-a-vis* Head Office was clearly established from the outset.

The advent of the party's regional organisation did not suddenly create an efficient organisational network. Far from it. With the exception of Scotland and London, there was no office accommodation available, and organisers had to work from their own homes. In addition, the organising areas were too large to allow detailed work at constituency level. Despite these inadequacies, the creation of nine regions, staffed by employees of the NEC, marked the party's first concerted attempt to establish a close rapport with the constituencies, since these national officials helped to stimulate party activity locally. In 1922 there were 2,400 divisional and local Labour Parties and trades councils in Britain, and by 1926 their numbers had increased to some 3,314.[9] The increase can be attributed, at least in part, to the work of these national field agents. Since all the organisers were making regular visits to constituencies, giving advice and help, 'personal touch between the parties in the constituencies and the National Staff is well maintained'.[10] In the Midlands, for example, the two organisers 'covered their wide area by visits, and a forward movement with regard to organisation has been started in several of the difficult positions of the Midland area'.[11] In the South-West region, the two organisers 'worked hard under difficult circumstances in this wide and

33

rural area. Much of the work has been of a propaganda character, but substantial progress is being made in the upbuilding of permanent organisation.'[12]

The early 1920s also witnessed the advent of regional conferences. The first conferences, held between July and December 1921, were convened in order to prepare constituencies for the pending General Election. They were invariably attended by the national agent and other national officials, as well as by the regional organisers. At the conferences, 'methods of organisation, electoral law and the services to the parties by the departments of the Head Office particularly in relation to an election campaign, were more fully explained and discussed'.[13] In addition, sometimes as many as 2,000 delegates from surrounding constituencies attended regional mass rallies at which the party leaders explained contemporary policy. The cost of these regional gatherings was borne by the National Executive Committee.

Lack of financial resources, rather than absence of political foresight, appears to have been responsible for the piecemeal development of the Labour Party's regional organisation. In particular, shortage of money was the root cause for the delay in establishing a regional structure for Wales. From 1917 onwards there were demands from various groups – notably the South Wales Labour Federation – for a Welsh advisory council on similar lines to that recently established in Scotland. The NEC examined the matter in some detail before concluding:

> On the basis of nationality Wales certainly appears to have a claim, and if devolution is decided upon, some organisation to give the Party in Wales a corporate means of expressing itself will be necessary. Whether the resources of the Party are equal to the strain and whether it is wise to anticipate devolution now, and whether a grant for an Advisory Council to Wales will act as an incentive to similar claims ... are matters that require serious consideration. ...[14]

For financial reasons, however, no council was established. In 1925 there were further resolutions in favour of establishing an advisory council for Wales but, once again, the Executive's answer was that 'the position of the Party's resources does not render the time opportune for such a development at present'.[15] The party's financial plight was emphasised by the fact that when Mr W. Holmes, Eastern Counties District Organiser, resigned his position in August 1928, the party could not afford to obtain a replacement.

It was not until August 1937, some twenty years after the initial soundings, that the South Wales Regional Council for Labour was finally established. [16] This was extended in 1947 to cover the whole of Wales and became the Welsh Council of Labour. [17] The establishment of this regional council produced tensions similar to those found earlier in Scotland. The NEC wanted to secure some influence over regional affairs and, to do this, it adopted a similar strategy to the one which had proved successful in Scotland. The constitution of this new regional council stipulated that: 'The Welsh District Organiser of the Labour Party shall act as Secretary to the Regional Council.' [18] The NEC was anxious to bring the industrial wing of the movement in South Wales, particularly the notoriously left-wing South Wales Miners Federation, into the mainstream of the party. It felt that greater co-ordination between the political and industrial wings of the movement was necessary for the Labour Party in South Wales to realise its full potential. As in Scotland, there was considerable opposition to the intrusion of the national party machine. At the 1937 Annual Conference, Councillor E. Allan Robson (Cardiff TC and LP) asserted that it was because of the somewhat divergent approach of the 'Council of Action' (an unofficial industrial movement dominated by the Miner's Federation of South Wales), on a number of issues, notably employment ('We got on the black books of the NEC'), that the NEC established the regional council, 'in order that it could gain greater influence over the Labour movement in Wales'. Robson drew attention to the fact that 'there is no democratic right to elect the Secretary. The Executive has been able to bring pressure to bear so that the District Organiser shall be permanently the Secretary of the Council.'[19] Replying for the NEC, Mr Arthur Jenkins MP asserted: 'It is sheer nonsense to say that the National Executive Council will dominate that body simply because a full-time official of the Labour Party is going to act as Secretary.'[20] Jenkins was probably correct in this assumption, but nevertheless, the hope seemed to be that, through the establishment of the Council, the Labour movement in Wales would be more easily influenced by the National Executive Committee.

Despite the financial constraints of the 1930s, the NEC began to develop a democratic regional structure to parallel its own organisational units. The industrial North-West with its high level of affiliated union membership was considered a viable starting-point. On 17 September 1938, the Lancashire and Cheshire Regional Council of the Labour Party was formed. [21] The desire to co-ordinate all affiliated party units within a given area stimulated the development of the Labour Party's regional organisation and the general position of the Labour Party's regional staff in the 1930s was well summarised in a note in *The Labour Organiser* of

February 1935. An interesting attitude to observe is that, despite the hostility of many constituencies towards regional organisers as the representatives of the National Executive Committee, many constituency parties were anxious to utilise the expertise which these national employees could provide:

> The national staff of the Labour Party is somewhat to be pitied these days. One or two of the present District and Women organisers date their appointments back to 1918, but the mapping out of the country into regions took place in 1924, when the appointment of a Man District Organiser and a Woman District Organiser to each of the nine districts took place. With one vacancy there are now eight Men District Organisers [including the Scottish Secretary] and nine Women Organisers. Since 1924 there has been a tremendous development of Party machinery and Party strength, but the [regional] staff remains at the same numerical strength. When the staff was first appointed it was, we believe, contemplated that offices would be opened, or at any rate that some development would take place as time went on, and the Party grew. Financial stringency has, however, entirely prevented any growth of staff or any developments of the kind indicated, but at the same time the expectations of the Movement, and the closer contact which long association entails, has considerably increased the calls upon, or the expectations of the staff, as it now stands. We are not voicing any complaint, but we write these lines because we feel that there are persons in the constituencies with a grumble, and we have heard those who have expressed a dissatisfaction because they cannot in their constituencies see the regional officers as often as they would like. [22]

On 10 January 1942, a Northern Regional Council was formed to cover the counties of Durham, Northumberland, and the North Riding of Yorkshire. In the following month, a Yorkshire Regional Council, incorporating the East and West Ridings, was established. In December 1942, the Midlands organising region was divided into the East and West Midlands, and a regional council was established in both these areas. [23] Referring to the development of these four new regional councils, the NEC observed, in 1942/3, that it 'had welcomed this activity with sympathy and approval, as the structure of the Party had been greatly strengthened by the influential delegations now functioning in the new bodies. . . . Although the whole country is not yet provided with this type of organisation, a pause in the creation of further councils is desirable. Action will be taken in other areas when local resources are sufficient to provide for the successful operation of the Councils therein.'[24]

In 1944, the NEC reported that 'when finance is available for the purpose, Regional Councils will be established in the Eastern Counties',[25] but lack of funds delayed further development of regional machinery until 1947, when the Eastern and Southern Regional Councils were formed.[26] With the establishment of the South-Western Regional Council in May 1948,[27] the whole of Britain was serviced by a network of regional councils, each served by a regional organiser appointed by the National Executive Committee.

The NEC strengthened its hold over the regions in the early 1950s. The 1951 Annual Conference Report stated:

> The NEC has had under review its financial relationship with the Regional Councils. In the light of experience, and with an increasing Regional Staff, it is necessary that added facilities in the form of accommodation and clerical assistance should be made available. During the formative years of the Regional Councils, the NEC has made grants but the responsibility for providing the facilities referred to has been that of the Regional Councils. A re-adjustment has now been made whereby the Regional Offices become the Regional Offices of the Labour Party, and responsibility is also being accepted for the clerical staff.[28]

The Lancashire and Cheshire Regional Council resisted this intrusion by Head Office. In its view, 'the best interests of the Party would be served by the [regional] office remaining the office of the Regional Council and under its direction'.[29] The NEC threatened to withhold its annual grant unless the regional executive agreed that the office should become the property of the NEC. It was this threat which finally forced the regional council to give way: 'It seems evident . . . that the Organisation Department (with the co-operation of the Finance Committee) has not hesitated to use economic sanctions to ensure that it retains full control of the affairs of the regional offices.'[30]

By 1950, therefore, there were ten regional councils functioning in England, Scotland and Wales. These, together with the London Labour Party, helped stimulate the development and co-ordination of party activity throughout the country. In 1951, however, a small but significant redistribution occurred: the large Southern Region, with 101 constituencies, was reduced to 73 constituencies with the surplus going to neighbouring regions. At the same time, the NEC decided, after negotiations with the London Labour Party and Middlesex Constituency Labour Parties, to merge the administrative county of London and the county of Middlesex, increasing the number of constituencies in London to 71. [31] Further changes, however, were soon proposed in London.

Wilson and Simpson: reform and change, 1955–68

In June 1955, following the party's General Election defeat earlier in the year, the Wilson Committee was appointed by the NEC to enquire into the general organisation of the party and to report back in September. [32] During its investigation, the Committee visited every regional office, meeting organisers and their deputies, then suggested in its report that: 'consideration might be given to the creation of a new Central Southern Area (corresponding to the Conservatives' Wessex Region) including Hampshire, Wiltshire, Berkshire, and Oxfordshire, or perhaps a new (North of the Thames) Home Counties Area covering Middlesex, Bedfordshire, Hertfordshire, and Buckinghamshire'. It also proposed that: 'The question of sub-regional offices in Wales and Scotland might also be reconsidered.' [33]

By 1957, the NEC had agreed to establish a new region, with a full complement of organisers, incorporating the 54 constituencies in the counties of Bedfordshire, Buckinghamshire, Berkshire, Hertfordshire, Oxfordshire, and Middlesex. But this decision split the counties concerned: 'Approximately half of them approved the proposals and half opposed the proposals.' [34] In view of this, the NEC decided not to proceed with the establishment of a new regional council, but to leave the parties, trade unions and other bodies to continue their affiliation with existing regional councils. However, it was decided to regard the area as a new organising region in the charge of a regional organiser. 'It is believed that this arrangement, while not disturbing existing regional ties, will enable a better organising service to be given.' [35] A new organising area was therefore established without a regional council, the constituencies concerned remaining affiliated to adjacent regional councils. This new organising region, Northern Home Counties, was formally established on 1 January 1959.

The Labour Party's second major organisational survey in the post-war years was completed in 1968. In November 1966, a small committee of enquiry had been set up by the NEC to 'enquire into Party organisation at all levels'. [36] One of the Committee's three working parties was concerned with regional organisation, and the final report observed:

> The creation of the Greater London Council made necessary the creation of corresponding Party machinery. In our interim report we

proposed that this should take the form of a Greater London Regional Council. Our proposal meant not only that the London Labour Party would disappear and its place be taken by a regional council, but also that there would have to be changes in the boundaries of the adjacent regions from which constituencies had been transferred to Greater London. [37]

The Committee proposed that the Northern Home Counties organising region be abolished and that its constituencies be returned to the regions in which they had previously belonged. It also recommended that Peterborough be transferred from the East Midlands Region to the Eastern Region, and that the Westmorland constituency be transferred from the North-Western Region to the Northern Region. [38]

At a consultative conference held at Hemel Hempstead on 16 November 1968, strong views were expressed in support of a proposal that the Northern Home Counties should remain an organising area and, in addition, that it should have its own regional council. At its meeting on 27 November, the NEC considered a detailed report of this consultation and determined: 'that (1) the Northern Home Counties Organising Area be abolished as recommended by the Enquiry Committee; (2) the constituency parties and County Federations in Bedfordshire and Hertfordshire shall be part of the Eastern Regional Council and be serviced by the Eastern Region Organising Staff; and (3) the constituency parties and County Federations in Berkshire, Buckinghamshire and Oxfordshire shall be part of the Southern Regional Council and will be serviced by the Southern Region Organising Staff. These new arrangements come into force from the 1st January 1969.' [39]

The recommendations of the Report of the Committee of Enquiry into Party Organisation provided the basis for reorganisation in the capital. On 31 March 1968, the Greater London Regional Council of the Labour Party was established, encompassing a population of 8 million people. The NEC divided the Greater London region into two areas, north and south, each with a team of three organisers: a regional organiser and two assistants, one of whom also dealt with youth organisation while the other dealt with women's organisation. This team of six organisers was directly responsible to the General Secretary of the Greater London Regional Council. Mr L. Sims, formerly Assistant National Agent of the Labour Party, became the first general secretary of the new council. [40]

The development of the Greater London Regional Council involved the dismantling of the old London Labour Party, which caused hostility, especially among the left-wing constituencies in inner London. The focus of the grievances, as in Scotland and Wales many years earlier, was the replacement of a secretary chosen by, and responsible to, the London Labour Party, by someone selected and employed by the NEC. The left-wing groups, in particular, did not want an official from Transport House running their affairs. Unlike the regional councils, the London Labour Party had always selected and employed its own secretary, and not unnaturally, many constituencies wanted to retain this privilege. The NEC, however, refused to allow this, although it did concede that 'the General Secretary and the Assistant Secretary shall be appointed by the National Executive Committee in consultation with the Executive Committee [of the Greater London Regional Council]'. [41] When the first two general secretaries were appointed, the Council's chairman merely attended the selection conference in an *ex-officio* capacity. He had no voting powers at the conference.

Conclusion

As well as the more obvious reasons for the establishment of regional organisation – namely the need to develop constituency organisation and to establish 'in every part of the country a complete liaison between co-operatives, Trade Unions, and the Constituency Labour Parties' [42] – the development of a regional network has also served to strengthen national party influence at the local level. In September 1974, the Labour Party employed a total of 38 regional organisers and assistant regional organisers in England, Scotland and Wales. In addition, the National Executive Committee also employ a general secretary and assistant secretary in Greater London. [43] The twelve organising regions created by the Labour Party each have their own democratic structures, with the exception of London North and South, which, as in the Conservative Party, combine to elect a regional council to serve the whole region.

The development of the Labour Party's regional organisation has produced tensions not unlike those found in the Conservative Party many years earlier. The NEC has, however, remained firmly in control throughout the development of the party's regional structure; it has not been forced to grant concessions to the democratic organisation in the way that the Conservative Party leadership was pressurised into weakening its control over the area structure at the turn of the century. Each regional office is a branch of Transport House and the NEC in the same way that each Conservative area office is a branch of Central Office and the party leadership, and the Labour Party's regional organisers serve as the field administrative officers of the National Executive Committee.

Notes

[1] F. Bealey and H. Pelling, *Labour and Politics 1900–1906*, London 1958, p. 239.

[2] 1913 Labour Party Annual Conference Report, p. 8.

[3] 1914 Labour Party Annual Conference Report, p. 33.

[4] 1919 Labour Party Annual Conference Report, p. 33.

[5] Ibid., pp. 33, 34.

[6] 1920 Labour Party Annual Conference Report, p. 18.

[7] 1921 Labour Party Annual Conference Report, pp. 33, 34.

[8] 1920 Labour Party Annual Conference Report, p. 18.

[9] 1922 Labour Party Annual Conference Report, p. 50, and 1926 Labour Party Annual Conference Report, p. 3.

[10] 1922 Labour Party Annual Conference Report, p. 50.

[11] Ibid., p. 51.

[12] Ibid., p. 51.

[13] 1922 Labour Party Annual Conference Report, p. 53.

[14] 1920 Labour Party Annual Conference Report, p. 17.

[15] 1925 Labour Party Annual Conference Report, p. 44.

[16] 'The first meeting of the Executive Committee was held on Saturday 28th August 1937.' See First South Wales Regional Council Annual Report, p. 13.

[17] 1948 Welsh Council of Labour Annual Report, p. 13.

[18] South Wales Regional Council of the Labour Party, Rules and Constitution. Clause XIV.

[19] 1937 Labour Party Annual Conference Report, p. 225.

[20] Ibid., p. 225.

[21] Lancashire and Cheshire Regional Council, First Annual Report. R.T. McKenzie in *British Political Parties* makes a minor mistake concerning the origins of regional councils: 'The first two regional councils of the Labour Party were those established in 1938, one for Lancashire and Cheshire, and the other for Wales' (p. 531). In fact, the Scottish Advisory Council was established in 1914, the South Wales Regional Council in 1937, and the Lancashire and Cheshire Regional Council in September 1938.

[22] *The Labour Organiser,* no. 164, February 1935, p. 21. Author's brackets.

[23] In the East Midlands, preliminary conferences were held on 5

December 1942 and 13 February 1943, for the purpose of establishing the Regional Council. (See East Midlands Regional Council, First Annual Report.)

[24] 1943 Labour Party Annual Conference Report, p. 30.

[25] 1944 Labour Party Annual Conference Report, p. 14.

[26] 1948 Labour Party Annual Conference Report, pp. 11 and 14.

[27] The first annual meeting of the South-Western Regional Council was held on 8 May 1948 (see first Annual Report).

[28] 1951 Labour Party Annual Conference Report, p. 15.

[29] 1953 Lancashire and Cheshire Regional Council, Annual Report, p.3.

[30] R.T. McKenzie, op.cit., p. 14.

[31] 1951 Labour Party Annual Conference Report, p. 14.

[32] 1955 Labour Party Annual Conference Report, p. 63.

[33] Ibid., p. 69.

[34] 1958 Labour Party Annual Conference Report, p. 17.

[35] Ibid. (NEC Report), p. 17.

[36] *Report of the Committee of Enquiry into Party Organisation,* The Labour Party, 1968, p. 17.

[37] Ibid., p. 17.

[38] Ibid., p. 18.

[39] Information from a circular letter sent by the National Agent (dated 6.12.68) to Constituency Parties and County Federations in the Northern Home Counties organising area. See also, S. Barker, 'Changes in some of our Regional Boundaries', *Labour Organiser,* 1969, pp. 28, 29.

[40] Mr L. Sims retired in 1970. He was replaced by the Assistant General Secretary in London, Mr R. Delafield.

[41] Greater London Regional Council of the Labour Party, Rules and Standing Orders, 1969, Clause X. Author's brackets.

[42] Morgan Phillips, Labour Party General Secretary, at 1949 Annual Conference. See Annual Report, p. 134.

[43] Information from H.R. Underhill, National Agent of the Labour Party, 9 September 1974.

3 The National/Regional Relationship

Introduction

As we have seen, both the Conservative and Labour Parties have established networks of regional offices upon which the respective leaderships have devolved administrative work. The devolution of administrative workload, however, is not identical to the decentralisation of administrative power. In both parties, all important organisational initiatives are taken nationally. Regional organisers and area agents implement these initiatives locally. In this context, Professor H. Jacob has asserted that:

> Every regime faces the troublesome task of making certain that its policies are translated into action rather than remaining paper mandates. This requires stationing government officials outside the capital, that is, in the field. Such field officials must be given enough flexibility to carry out programmes as they see fit, so that they can meet the particular problems of their locale. At the same time the central government must retain sufficient control over its field agents to assure fully-fledged execution of national programmes, for they are removed from direct contact with central officials.[1]

Regional organisers and area agents are employed and directed by their respective party leaderships. Some discussion of the personnel working at the regional level is provided at the outset of this chapter as background material to its major theme — the relationship of regional organisers and area agents with their respective head offices.

The professional side of the Conservative Party's organisation, Central Office, has close links with the National Union, both centrally and in the areas. Nationally, the Director of Organisation also acts as honorary secretary of the National Union. In the same way, a Central Office area agent always acts as the honorary secretary of his area council[2] and its committees. In addition, the various departments at Central Office are linked with the National Union through the Union's advisory committees. Labour Party regional organisers, like Conservative area agents, are appointed nationally, but are employed by the party's National Executive Committee and not by the Parliamentary leadership. The formal relationship between regional organisers and their regional councils is clearly laid down. The constitution of the Lancashire and Cheshire Regional Council of the Labour Party is typical in stating that: 'The North-West District Organiser of the Labour Party shall act as Secretary to the Regional Council.'[3] Regional organisers, like area agents, serve the party leadership, not only by liaising directly with the centre on a wide variety of matters, but also by servicing the democratic organisation at the regional level and thereby providing a degree of supervision.

Personnel at the regional and area level

Very little data is available on the origins, education and past careers of professional party organisers. In January 1971, the author sent a questionnaire to all regional organisers and area agents to determine their backgrounds. The following brief profiles of regional and area organising staff are based on the responses to the questionnaire.

A typical Labour Party regional organiser attended elementary school and left at the age of 14. He then went into industry and, in his spare time, attended technical college or else studied a correspondence course. He joined the party at 18, having been brought up in a family in which his parents were politically active. After working in a voluntary capacity with the local party he entered the full-time agency service at the age of 32. He then served as party agent in two constituencies for a total of about 6 years. At the age of 40, he was appointed assistant regional organiser, remaining at this level for some 6 years, then, roughly 12 years after first entering the full-time agency service, he became a regional organiser.

The average Conservative Party area agent attended either grammar or public school until the age of 17, after which he had no form of further education. He joined the party at 21, coming from a family background with little or no involvement in politics. He did not engage in any voluntary work for the local party but spent 6½ years in the army, followed by a short time in outside employment, before entering the agency service at the age of 26. He had an average of some 2½ constituency agencies, totalling just over 9 years, before becoming a deputy area agent at the age of 40. He spent 3 years as a deputy before becoming an area agent, some 13½ years after first entering the agency service. He will probably have served as area agent in two areas, spending about 6 years in the first and 7½ years to date in his current area.

The national/regional relationship in the Labour Party

In the Labour Party, the major organisational initiatives are taken by the National Executive Committee or, more specifically, by the Organisation Department at Transport House. The role of the regional organiser is to work within nationally determined frameworks of action, applying national policies to his region, and utilising local knowledge where appropriate. Some recent examples serve to illustrate the nature of the relationship between the party's head office and the regional staff.

Firstly, regional organisers are given periodic directives concerning the selection of prospective Parliamentary candidates. In May 1971, for example, the national agent sent the following letter to all regional organisers:

> The NEC has decided that the selection of prospective Parliamentary candidates in the non-Labour constituencies and in those constituencies where the present Labour MP has intimated that he will not be seeking re-election should be dealt with on the basis of priorities. Will you please let me have as quickly as possible the list of constituencies within your region in which you propose that the first elections should take place on a priority basis. Meanwhile you are requested not to arrange to meet any constituency party to discuss selection procedure and a draft timetable until approval is given to your proposals for priorities.[4]

Regional organisers are usually given a time limit by which all selections must be completed, but the precise order of the selection conferences is frequently left to the discretion of regional organisers, on the understanding that politically marginal constituencies must always receive priority. The relatively close supervision exercised by the national agent over regional organisers can be seen from the above quotation.

Secondly, at strategic times — notably just before an expected General Election — regional organisers are frequently instructed, at one of their half-yearly staff conferences, to concentrate their resources on marginal constituencies. Regional office concentration on critical constituencies between February and October 1974 reflected such a national directive. The precise amount of time to be devoted to each constituency is left to the discretion of the individual organiser, although, should the national agent feel that a regional organiser is allocating resources incorrectly, he will invariably send a directive requiring a change.

Thirdly, directives to organise membership campaigns within the regions are received relatively frequently at regional office. Once again, the precise techniques to be adopted are left to the discretion of the regional organiser, provided that his detailed plans are compatible with the nationally determined framework of action.

Finally, regional organisers often receive instructions from Transport House to organise policy conferences. These meetings are imposed on the regions by the NEC, and regional organisers must involve themselves with the detailed administrative work associated with staging such conferences. One such series of regional conferences was entitled 'The Policies of the Labour Government' and, between January and November 1967, the North-West Regional Office had to organise thirteen of these conferences.[5] In the twelve months from June 1967, there were nineteen policy conferences on a wide variety of topics in the West Midlands Region,[6] while in the East Midlands fourteen conferences were organised during the same period.[7]

As the field agents of the Labour Party's National Executive Committee, regional organisers fulfil a wide variety of roles, which can be illustrated with reference to specific examples.

Regional organisers must submit all local government election returns to Transport House in a particular format and at a predetermined time so that party headquarters is in a position to make informed comments on the results to both press and television as quickly as possible. In addition, detailed reports on all local government by-elections must be submitted to Head Office by the regional organiser.

Regional organisers are given detailed instructions by the national agent at all Parliamentary by-elections. On occasions, a regional organiser is obliged to act as election agent in preference to the local agent. A representative from Head Office attends all by-elections to offer advice on organisational matters which a regional organiser is almost duty-bound to accept. Transport House also requires regional organisers to report at regular intervals on the work of constituency agents employed in the National Agency Scheme.[8] These reports are detailed, containing information on the past, present and probable future work of the agents in question. Until March 1971, these reports had to be submitted monthly, but, since then, Transport House has only demanded quarterly reports.

Regional organisers are directed to organise training meetings for key officers at both general and local government elections. Funds for these meetings are provided by party headquarters and frequently a Head Office representative is present. In matters such as these, regional organisers are afforded little discretion. As the employees of the NEC they must abide by the instructions of the national agent's department at Transport House.

Regional organisers represent the National Executive Committee in a variety of ways at the constituency level. According to the Party Constitution, the NEC must be represented at all conferences connected with the selection of prospective Parliamentary candidates. It is obviously not deemed practical for someone from Transport House to travel to selection conferences throughout the country when there is an official representative within relatively easy reach of most constituencies. Often four visits by a regional organiser or one of his assistants are necessary before a candidate is finally selected. A constituency party cannot legitimately select a prospective Parliamentary candidate without a representative from the National Executive Committee being present.[9] In practice, the NEC representative is invariably the regional organiser.

The redistribution of Parliamentary constituency boundaries in 1970 involved regional organisers in a considerable amount of work in their role as representatives of the NEC. In 1970/71 regional organisers represented the NEC at the various meetings associated with the closing down of old, and the establishment of new, constituency parties. Besides usually writing the minutes of the establishment conferences, regional organisers frequently sent out the notices announcing selection conferences in those constituencies with sitting Labour members. Initially, regional organisers met existing constituency officers to discuss the basis of representation for the establishment meetings in the newly created constituency parties; they discussed the assets and liabilities of the old parties; they dealt with the credentials of the delegates appointed to the establishment meetings. In these and similar matters, regional staff acted as the representatives of the NEC, ensuring that all detailed arrangements were in line with nationally determined criteria.

From time to time, the NEC instructs regional organisers to conduct enquiries on its behalf. These enquiries usually involve matters such as the expulsion of an individual member by a constituency party. At such enquiries, the regional organiser is always assisted by members of his regional council (see Chapter 7). Regional organisers also invariably represent the National Executive Committee at agency selection meetings, as constituency parties are unable to select full-time agents without an NEC representative being present.

Regional organisers are, therefore, allowed some scope to exercise initiative. Essentially, however, they act as the field agents of the NEC and, as such, are subject to close supervision by the centre. The degree of supervision is indicated by the 'reporting-in' system adopted by the Labour Party.

Each regional organiser is obliged to report to the national agent on each visit (however brief) made to a constituency party, local party, trade union, or some other organisation. These reports are submitted on forms

47

supplied by the Organisation Department at Transport House, and most regional organisers send between 300 and 400 reports to Head Office each year. This device is, of course, designed to keep the centre informed, in some detail, of the organisational situation at the constituency and local party levels throughout the country. Such reports are frequently part of an established field administrative network.

The Wilson Committee on Party Organisation (1955) deemed the reports unnecessary, but their use has continued. Wilson was concerned

> ... at the volume of what we consider to be largely unnecessary paperwork. Reports from regional staff on visits are pouring into Transport House at the rate of at least 7,000 per annum. The task of reading (and dictating) the reports is in our view a wasteful use of headquarters and regional staff. Moreover, the very existence of the system creates a wrong relationship between head office and the regions based on a degree of over-centralisation which we should expect to find in a minor department of the War Office rather than in a great national Party. [10]

Transport House has, however, firmly resisted the notion of monthly reports. The system of reporting every visit on a pre-printed form has enabled the centre to know in some detail what its field agents are doing. The centre has always been eager to retain the control which a system of reporting-in provides, and although this system is resented at the regional level protests against it do not appear to have made any significant impact. [11]

The Wilson Report also commented on the infrequency of staff conferences:

> When the last conference was held, in June 1954, it was overloaded with an agenda of some 34 items, reflecting the excessive intervals between conferences. We find, for instance, one morning session organised as follows:
>
> 9.30–11 a.m.   Marginal Constituencies
>
> (a) Work accomplished and proposed plans
> (b) Appointment of agents (Document)
> (c) Subsidised literature
> (d) NALSO Canvassing Teams 1954
> (e) Postal Vote Canvassers
> (f) Training of Agents and Key Workers

11.15–12.45 p.m.   Party Organisation

    (a)   Membership (Document)
    (b)   TU affiliations – National, Regional and Local
    (c)   Co-operative affiliations (Document)
    (d)   Constituency Party Finance (Document)
    (e)   Agency in General (Document)
    (f)   League of Youth

Wilson remarked: 'With such an agenda it is clear that there is no time for discussion or any two-way exchange of ideas: in general the time provided for each item could not allow for much more than a statement by the national officer concerned.' [12]

By 1971 there was more contact between regional and national officials. There were, on average, two meetings each year between regional staff and the national agent's department as well as one meeting incorporating assistant regional organisers. Nevertheless, the frequency of the meetings was offset by the still overcrowded agendas, which permitted little meaningful two-way flow of information. The following agenda, from the Regional Organisers Consultation held at Transport House on 29 March 1971 from 11 a.m. to 4.30 p.m. illustrates this point:

1   Parliamentary Redistribution
    (a)   Establishment of new constituency parties
    (b)   Endorsement of rules
    (c)   Resettlement of MP's
    (d)   Selection of Parliamentary Candidates
    (e)   Finance, Outstanding Accounts (Mr D. Richards)
2   Local Government Reform
(Ann Carlton, Local Government Officer, will attend this session)
    (a)   Conservative Proposals (doc. Rd 78)
    (b)   Boundaries, Functions and Politics (doc. Rd 78)
    (e)   Summary of RO's Analysis of Political Implications (doc.)
3   Local Government Elections
    (a)   Schedules
    (b)   Results
    (c)   Qualifications for Candidates (doc. MMSO)
4   Consultations with Labour Groups
5   Subsidies for Schools on Party Organisation
6   By-elections
7   Closure 4.30 p.m. [13]

The overcrowded agenda was, then, just as evident in 1971 as it had been in 1954 and there was still only time for little more than a brief statement by the national officer, with the result that information flowed only one way.

The national/area relationship in the Conservative Party

In the Conservative Party, each of the eleven area offices acts as a branch of Central Office. In 1949, the *Final Report of the Committee on Party Organisation* (The Maxwell-Fyfe Report), observed: 'The composition of the Area Office . . . in contrast to the constituency offices, *is under the direct control of Central Office.'* [14] The relationship between Central Office and the areas was examined by the Maxwell-Fyfe Committee, which reported as follows:

> Is the Central Office agent under the orders of Central Office or of the Area Chairman? The Central Office agent is directly under the orders of the General Director, but in practice the Area Chairman and the Central Office agent both work together harmoniously in the pursuance of a common task. . . . It has been suggested that the Area Agents should be appointed from a panel approved by the Executive Committee of the National Union. We do not concur with this suggestion, but the Area Chairman should always be consulted before the appointment of any new Area Agent. [15]

Area agents administer a variety of national campaigns, of which the periodic membership drives, the occasional national fund-raising campaigns and the annual contracting-out campaign are examples. Broad strategies are announced nationally and area agents implement these directives, taking into account the local situation. Area agents must also deal with certain essential matters at the constituency level. The closing down of old, and the setting up of new, parties following the 1970 Conservative Government's Redistribution Act is a specific example. In this matter, area agents were given detailed instructions by Central Office concerning procedure, but, at the same time, they were allowed flexibility over the precise timing, provided that the whole operation was completed by 31 March 1972.

Much of the preliminary work associated with the appointment of full-time constituency association agents is handled at the area level, thereby relieving Central Office of routine administration. The role played by area offices in the allocation of speakers for constituency and branch meetings again eases pressure on Central Office. In the West Midlands

Area, for example, large numbers of speakers have been allocated by the area office in recent years: 1965/6 395; 1966/7 390; 1967/8 369; 1968/9 436. [16] Routine work is left to the 'branches' of Central Office.

Central Office relies on its area agents for much of the information for the extensive results service which it provides during local government elections. During General Elections, contact between Central Office and the area agents is particularly close. During the 1970 General Election, area staff were instructed to telephone the Director of Organisation at a predetermined time each day. 'Intelligence' material was fed to Central Office from the constituencies via the area agents, thus allowing unimportant information to be sifted at the area level. The detailed nature of the control exercised by Central Office over its field agents was well illustrated during this particular General Election when area agents were instructed to obtain six specimen copies of all opposition literature in each constituency and send it to Head Office where it could be examined in detail. This was not a request — it was a command. [17]

The minutes of every area committee are sent to London, thereby enabling Head Office to follow through any points of interest and to keep informed on developments in each provincial area. In contrast to the Labour Party, however, there is no formal system of 'reporting-in' to Central Office on every assignment. The 'reporting-in' system in the Conservative Party is much more flexible. Although each area agent is required to report to Central Office about Parliamentary selection conferences and agency selection conferences, an experienced area agent will only transmit information to Central Office when he feels that headquarters should be informed, given the likelihood of enquiries on the matter from elsewhere. The contrast with the Labour Party should not, however, be drawn too sharply. Central Office is linked to each area office by a telex system. One could argue that this network (not established in the Labour Party until February 1974) has facilitated closer, albeit more informal, contact between Central Office and the area offices than has been obtainable through the Labour Party's extensive form-filling system.

By moving the area agents round from area to area every eight years or so, the Conservative Party conforms to accepted field administrative practice. This prevents an agent from becoming too attached to a locality, at the expense of his loyalty to the centre. In the West Midlands, however the area agent, Mr J. Galloway, has been in the area since 1956 and, it seems, will remain there until his retirement some two years hence. Personal reasons have dictated this unusually long stay in a single region. Galloway has proved an exception to the rule by being extremely independent, and has raised, for example, a regional fund with which he has financed a series of organisational innovations in the area. This project was not received very enthusiastically at Central Office. In 1970, Galloway reported:

> For some years I have been able to launch the following schemes in selected constituencies:
>
> (a) Poster boards for use during the General Election campaign.
>
> (b) Letters from Members of Parliament to all electors on the 'B' list on House of Commons note paper in House of Commons envelopes, sealed.
>
> (c) In the year immediately before the election, letters to new young voters.
>
> (d) Letters to association members regarding postal votes.
>
> (e) Appropriate communications to selected opinion-forming personnel. [18]

In addition, Galloway financed propaganda newspapers for a time in selected marginal constituencies. Despite Galloway's relatively independent line with Central Office on some issues, all area agents have the same basic relationship with the centre. They are field administrative agents for Central Office and are accountable to the party leadership.

Conservative area agents are used far more widely than Labour Party regional organisers for taking soundings of opinion in the country. This 'intelligence' service is, of course, used most intensively during general elections, but even during non-election periods area agents are occasionally instructed by Central Office to take soundings of opinion at local level. 'Intelligence' in the Conservative Party assumes far greater significance at area level than it does at the regional level in the Labour Party. The relative abundance of full-time constituency agents in the Conservative Party enables area agents to concentrate on intelligence work, while their Labour Party opposite numbers are, because of the lack of skilled agents at the local level, involved in much more routine organisational work. [19] In the transmission of ideas upwards from local to national levels, area agents are more fully utilised than Labour Party regional organisers.

Conclusion

Within the nationally determined frameworks of action, both regional organisers and area agents are afforded some initiative. While the relationship of Conservative area agents with Central Office differs slightly from that of regional organisers with Transport House, the essential similarity remains with both parties employing their regional staff to act as field agents for the respective leaderships. The major reason for the development and maintenance of a network of field administration in the Labour and Conservative Parties has, however, been administrative convenience. The degree of control exercised by the respective head offices over their regional and area officials does not indicate that the two parties are highly centralised, and there is no evidence to show that the chain of command extends beyond the regional and area organisers to the constituency parties. In both parties, constituency associations, proud of their relative autonomy, frequently ignore directives from the regional offices as will be shown in Chapters 4 and 5. The chain of command from the centre does not extend beyond the regional level.

Notes

[1] *German Administration since Bismarck,* New Haven and London 1963, p. 1.
[2] See Chapter 7 for discussion of the democratic framework at the regional/area level.
[3] Lancashire and Cheshire Regional Council of the Labour Party, Rules, Constitution and Standing Orders, p. 8.
[4] Document sent to all regional organisers by the national agent. Reference: NAD/RO/8/5/71.
[5] 1968 North-West Regional Council Annual Report, p. 7.
[6] 1968 West Midlands Regional Council Annual Report, p. 4.
[7] 1968 East Midlands Regional Council Annual Report, p. 5.
[8] The National Agency Scheme was established by the NEC in 1969. In September 1974 there were 41 constituency party agents employed in the scheme. A proportion of the salaries of these agents was paid by the NEC. In return, the national party headquarters required to know in some detail the nature of the work carried out by these agents at the constituency party level.
[9] The Labour Party, Constitution and Rules, Section D, Clause XI, pp. 13, 14.
[10] *Interim Report of the Sub-Committee on Party Organisation* (The Wilson Report), 1955 Labour Party Annual Conference Report, p. 68.
[11] In 1967, for example, the East Midlands Regional Organiser and his two deputies sent Transport House a total of 925 reports on visits completed.

[12] *Interim Report of the Sub-Committee on Party Organisation,* op.cit., p. 67.

[13] Agenda, Regional Organisers' Consultation, 29 March 1971. The conference chairman was the national agent.

[14] *Final Report of the Committee on Party Organisation,* The National Union, London 1949, p. 20 (author's italics).

[15] Ibid., p. 21.

[16] 1965–70 West Midlands Area Council Annual Reports.

[17] This task was not as simple as it might appear. In the West Midlands, for example, where opposition literature often proved difficult to obtain, typists from area office were sent in search of the necessary quota of leaflets, disguised as students.

[18] J. Galloway, Report to the half yearly meeting of the West Midlands Area Council, 24 October 1970.

[19] In September 1974, the Labour Party employed 120 constituency agents compared with 375 in the Conservative Party. Labour figures for Great Britain; Conservative figures for England and Wales only.

4 The Constituency/Regional Relationship in Action

Regional and area staff are involved in a wide variety of work as the field agents of their respective head offices. While some of this work affects all constituencies (such as that involved in the selection of prospective Parliamentary candidates), much of it is highly selective, focusing on constituencies with, for example, weak organisation, a critical financial situation, an internal crisis, or a by-election. Because the range of work is vast, a classification has been adopted to bring order out of chaos. Work at the regional and area level is considered under the following four headings: regulatory, conciliatory, advisory and servicing. The work which regional and area staff are specifically concerned with during General Elections is dealt with separately in Chapter 8.

Regulatory

Selection of Parliamentary candidates

Regional and area staff act, in a number of matters, as the representatives of their respective head offices and try to ensure that approved procedures are adhered to at the constituency level. The regulatory role played by regional and area staff in the process of selecting prospective Parliamentary candidates is extremely important. According to Professor Austin Ranney:

> The selection of parliamentary candidates is one of the least discussed and most recondite of the interlocking mysteries that make up the British system of Government. . . . Labour regional organisers play, if anything, an even more active role in candidate selection than do Conservative area agents.[1]

Ranney quotes one regional organiser thus:

> Every now and again Hugh Gaitskell, who knows me and trusts me, tells me privately, 'Look, young X is a very able chap and we could use him to good purpose in the House. Would you see what you can

do for him? When he does, I review the situation in all the parties in my region carefully. If I see one that is winnable, and that has officers who are good friends of mine, I drive over and have a quiet chat with them. Usually they can at least guarantee that my man will get on the short list, and sometimes they can also see to it that he is the only able man on the list. After that, of course, it's up to the man himself to convince the selection conference that he's what they want. But they usually do rather well. Ranney adds, 'This particular organiser has scored several triumphs, but by no means all of his eleven colleagues have been equally successful.'[2]

While this appraisal is rather too simple, it does provide a useful insight into the informal procedures which operate at the regional level. Ranney, unlike Rush,[3] concentrates on more than the selection conference itself. By focusing on the final selection conferences, it is hardly surprising to find Rush concluding that regional organisers are little more than procedural and constitutional advisers. Rush observes that

In practice the regional organiser or other NEC representative holds a watching brief over selection meetings, acting as a guide on procedure and a guarantor of the efficacy of the selection and, as the assistant national organiser pointed out in 1956, 'no officer or representative of the NEC should be allowed to speak on the merits or demerits of the nominee'. (*Labour Organiser,* January 1956, p. 13.)[4]

Throughout his analysis Rush views the role of the regional organiser in purely formal terms. In doing so, he fails to recognise the informal backroom manoeuvring which invariably accompanies selection. While the formal role is important, it is wrong to give the impression that regulations are the sole concern of a regional organiser at this particular time. The formal role must be seen in its proper perspective.

A regional organiser is closely involved in discussions at the constituency level concerning the timetable of selection. Throughout the selection process, he acts as the representative of the NEC, checking procedure, ensuring the validity of nomination forms, appointing delegates and in every way checking that the procedure outlined by the NEC is followed as closely as possible. Rush examines three selection conferences in some detail: Newark, Bromley and Birkenhead. All three were prior to the 1964 General Election.

Referring to the Bromley selection Rush observes:

The Regional Organiser for the Southern Region of the Labour Party, who acted as the representative of the NEC, confined his role to that of procedural adviser. Only once, when a question was asked about sponsorship, did he make a categorical statement . . . there was no sign that the CLP had had any great experience of selection and the local officials relied heavily on the Regional Organiser for advice.[5]

In both Newark and Birkenhead the regional organisers were seen to play similar procedural roles.

There is, however, some evidence to indicate that regional organisers occasionally play a part in securing nominations for particular candidates. Often constituency parties in safe Conservative seats contact regional office for the names of possible candidates to fill out a short list for a forthcoming selection conference. Indeed, on occasions, complete short lists are provided by regional office. Numerous candidates in 'hopeless' Labour constituencies have related how they were telephoned by regional office and asked to fly the flag in a particular constituency.

Far more important than this, however, is the influence which certain regional organisers have exerted in safe Labour or marginal constituencies. Some regional organisers have taken it upon themselves to 'place' their own nominees at strategic times in recent years – notably during the CDS/Victory for Socialism squabble in the early 1960s and during the pro/anti common market debate within the party in the early 1970s. By cultivating over many years informal contacts at the constituency level, regional organisers are frequently able to guarantee that their nominee is the most able person on a short list and therefore fairly certain of being chosen as prospective Parliamentary candidate. It would be invidious to provide names of sitting Members of Parliament who have secured nomination in this way, but, in one region alone, about half the sitting members obtained their seats, whether knowingly or not, through the informal behind-the-scenes manoeuvring of regional staff – notably the regional organiser.

It requires years of contact with ward parties and key notables in a constituency before a regional organiser is in a position to put forward names of potential candidates to opinion leaders at the constituency level. The most 'successful' regional organisers have often been in a region over twenty years and have well-established contacts which can be utilised as and when required. No regional organiser can force a constituency party to adopt a particular candidate – indeed this would be a very ill-advised policy. He must rely on pressure behind the scenes, entirely the product of influence developed over many years, rather than authority enshrined in a party rule book. Influence rather than authority is the key note of regional activity and this is nowhere more true than during candidate selection.

It is alleged by some commentators that one of the most notable instances of regional intervention in the candidate selection process was at Lincoln in 1962 when Dick Taverne was chosen as prospective Parliamentary candidate to fight a by-election in the constituency.[6] A recent review of Taverne's book, *The Future of the Left*, has argued that:

> The short list of candidates prepared by the Lincoln Party's Executive Committee, in conjunction with the Labour Party's East Midlands regional organiser (himself a key undercover worker for CDS), contained no unilateralist or Left candidate ... Taverne's selection as the Labour candidate for Lincoln is just one example of the attempts by CDS, in this case successful, to manipulate the candidate selection process to its advantage. *In its national campaign it had the support of the majority of the Labour Party's regional organisers, persons with a key role in the candidate selection process.*[7]

According to Seyd, seven of the twelve regional organisers were sympathetic to CDS in 1961. Certainly, even if this figure is somewhat exaggerated, at least three regional organisers at this time wore their hearts on their sleeves during the CDS/Victory for Socialism battle within the Labour Party.[8] Whatever the precise number of 'undercover' agents for the CDS in the early 1960s, however, it is important to recognise that the role played by regional organisers in candidate selection is determined almost entirely through the informal contacts and respect built up over many years.

Turning to the Conservative Party, M.D. Rush provides a useful analysis of the role of area agents at a selection conference and examines Croydon Conservative Association prior to the 1964 General Election. At the selection meeting:

> The discussion which led to the final short-list was held after the last of the interviews. At the suggestion of the Central Office Area Agent, who attended the meetings of the selection committee in an advisory capacity, an immediate vote was taken to reduce the fifteen to a more manageable number. This resulted in a short-list of six names.
>
> The Area Agent again intervened and advised the Committee that their main consideration should be to select a short-list of persons whom they felt were 'best suited to the constituency *and not those*

who had impressed them most'. He went on to point out that 'a mistake was made at Orpington' where the selected candidate would have made an excellent MP but *'was not the right man for the constituency'*.[9] [Rush later notes:] Only where he gave *procedural* advice did the Area Agent urge a particular course upon the committee and his comments on the applicants were either non-committal or designed to ensure that justice was being done to a particular individual. There was no indication that he was attempting to secure the selection, or prevent the rejection of one or more of the applicants. Nor, during the short break that occurred, did the Area Agent attempt to exert any informal or indirect pressure.[10]

Formally, constituency associations are autonomous in the process of candidate selection. This was made clear by Mr Richard Sharples (Vice Chairman of the Party Organisation) in a debate at the 1968 Conservative Party Conference:

The choice of how you select a candidate and the choice of the methods which you adopt is yours, that of the constituency association, alone. We at Central Office are there to help constituencies if they ask us to do so. But I agree very much with one speaker. It would be quite wrong, and it has never been the policy of Central Office, certainly in recent times, to try to foist particular candidates upon constituencies. To do so would be not only wrong from our point of view but would be damning for the particular candidate whose chances were being advocated in that way.[11]

In theory, therefore, Conservative Party area agents only have a formal role to play in the selection of prospective Parliamentary candidates. In practice, however, there is frequently far greater activity at the area level. It would be naïve to imagine area staff standing by and watching candidates short-listed and adopted without any intervention on their part.

Area office influence is greatest at the preliminary and short-listing stages. One area agent asserted that 'you can usually get people on a short-list unless on paper they look very bad'. He added, however, that he would 'never try to influence the final decision'.[12] Another area agent maintained that he would deliberately expose the weakness in a candidate he was not keen on being adopted, and then he would persuade someone to ask a question to reveal the weakness.[13] Again, this area agent emphasised that the area staff often have a negative influence at the early stages of candidate selection, particularly when drawing up lists of candidates prior to the short-listing stage. He observed: 'We know who we do not want to stand and we have our favourites. It is not Webster and Grant (at Central Office) who dictate but it is we who simply put forward our prejudices in excluding or encouraging candidates.' [14]

It must be admitted that the area's role in candidate selection is often shrouded in secrecy, but there is a need to recognise the tremendous potential influence which regional and area staff can exert over the selection process. Although it would be unwise to claim too much influence for regional and area staff in the process of candidate selection, it would be equally wrong to underestimate the undoubted reality of informal influence at this level.

Linked with candidate selection is the re-nomination of sitting members. At the height of the Bevanite rebellion in the mid-1950s two constituency Labour parties tried to drop right-wing candidates but were prevented from doing so by Transport House — notably by the regional organisers. In June 1954, the General Management Committee of Liverpool Exchange Constituency Labour Party decided to dismiss their MP, Bessie Braddock, and it was left to the North-West regional organiser, R. Wallis, to inform the constituency party that it had acted unconstitutionally. Wallis told them that if they refused to re-adopt Mrs Braddock the NEC might be forced to disaffiliate the existing Exchange party and form a new one. Eventually the Exchange party was reluctantly persuaded to adopt Mrs Braddock. [15]

In 1955 a similar episode occurred at Coventry South when the constituency party refused to adopt Elaine Burton as candidate. The NEC refused to accept the sacking and eventually Miss Burton was re-adopted and re-elected in 1955. In both the Liverpool Exchange and the Coventry South instances, regional organisers played important roles as the representatives of Transport House. [16]

In 1974, Eddie Milne (Blyth) was not re-adopted by his constituency party to fight the February election and E. Griffiths (Sheffield Brightside) suffered a similar fate prior to the October 1974 General Election. Regional organisers, as the local representatives of the National Executive Committee, were inevitably very closely involved in these two controversies, ensuring that the rule book was followed by the constituency parties in question. A third regional organiser told me how he had been similarly involved in a constituency in his own region immediately before the same General Election. For him, the biggest triumph of all was settling the issue without the press or mass media realising that he had been involved. During the whole of the time the dispute raged, not one single newspaper contacted him for a statement. This illustrates how regional and area organisers work quietly behind the scenes in the process of candidate selection: few people realise they take any meaningful part in the process.

Selection of constituency agents

Regional organisers and area agents play a role in the appointment of full-time constituency party agents. No constituency Labour Party may advertise for a full-time agent without the prior approval of the regional organiser. A regional organiser must be satisfied that a constituency party is financially able to support an agent and will examine the financial statements and balance sheets of the party in question before giving approval to go ahead and advertise for an agent. The following report provides an indication of the nature of a regional investigation. It also illustrates the representations which a regional organiser frequently makes to Head Office. The report concerns a visit made by the West Midlands regional organiser to the Burton-on-Trent constituency Labour Party in May 1969:

> Their present financial position is as follows:
> Because they have cleared all their liabilities they are beginning to build up some funds and have a balance in their current account of £420.
> The freehold property they own has been renovated with the ground floor used for Party Offices and the upper floors used for five modern flatlets.
> There is £700 outstanding on the mortgage which has 15 years to run, but they are hoping to clear it completely long before that term of years.
> The flats bring in a weekly income of £18. 15s. 0d. and, after all outgoings including rates, mortgage repayments, Corporation tax etc., they are making about £200 a year profit from the property.
> They have a constituency tote realising a profit of £500 a year.
> They have built up their participation in the Golden Prize Club largely through the initiative of Ron Truman and will have an annual income of at least £200 a year from this source.
> There is a Labour Club in the Stapenhill ward within the Borough of Burton although this is not a Labour Party Club. Recently the ownership of the premises has been taken over by the Constituency Labour Party and the Club is paying £50 a year rent. There are good chances that this Club will become very prosperous and in consequence a higher rent is likely in the future.

In a normal voting pattern I am convinced that organisation would make all the difference in winning this seat.

A grant at a rate of £400 a year would make it certain that they could manage to start an agency and I hope such a grant would be possible.

With both the Candidate and the Treasurer ready to try all sorts of ideas this Party could become a very good example to many others. If the grant is available I have been authorised by the Party to arrange for the necessary advertisements for the vacancy. [17]

It is the regional organiser who arranges for the vacancy to be advertised. He must meet the constituency party executive committee to sift through the applications and to draw up a short-list. Informally, considerable manoeuvring invariably goes on behind the scenes, and one organiser remarked: 'We tout round quietly where we want someone badly for a constituency.' [18] Another regional organiser asserted: 'One has got to make sure the right people apply.'[19] Although, formally, a regional organiser must follow the various NEC directives at every stage of the selection process, the informal aspects of the job must be recognised at the same time.

A regional organiser will usually visit a new constituency agent and provide some guidelines about the job. Following the appointment of a new agent to Rushcliffe constituency in December 1969, the East Midlands regional organiser duly visited the agent: 'I discussed with him what I consider to be the priorities in organisation in the constituency. These were: (a) to build up the tote scheme; (b) the selection of County Council and Urban District Council candidates; and (c) training schemes for key workers.' [20] The provision of such advice is particularly marked in constituencies employing National Agency Scheme agents. [21]

Conservative Party area agents also play a role in the recruitment, training and deployment of constituency association agents. An aspiring constituency agent is usually put into contact with the area agent, who takes full particulars of each candidate, and if deemed suitable, these are sent to the Personnel Officer at Central Office, who is also secretary of the Agents' Examination Board. The candidate is then entered for the preliminary examination. Area agents frequently deliberately exaggerate the drawbacks of the agency service in order to deter weak candidates, so that an area agent will often ask a candidate with little experience of voluntary work in the party to spend some time in this capacity before entering the agency service. Candidates who pass the preliminary

62

examination are sent for training in a constituency, chosen jointly by the secretary of the Examination Board, and the area agent. It appears that the Examinations Secretary usually takes the advice of the area agent, although on occasions the area agent is overruled by the Head Office official. [22]

A constituency association requiring an agent usually contacts area office. The area agent arranges for an advertisement to be sent forward to the personnel officer at Central Office, who circulates the list of vacancies each week to those agents and constituency parties who have requested it. All applications are sent direct to Central Office and thence to the area agent who, in his turn, sends the names to a constituency association. Central Office will frequently suggest a preference to the area agent but, as in the selection of Parliamentary candidates, constituency associations can refuse to accept advice offered by the area.

Parliamentary redistribution

Regional organisers and area agents act as the representatives of their respective head offices in the work associated with Parliamentary redistribution. Redistribution is, of course, relatively infrequent. Since the last war there have been only two major redistributions, in 1948 and in 1970, although there were minor changes to constituency boundaries during the 1950s. During a redistribution, old parties must be closed down and new ones established. Regional organisers and area agents supervise the work, ensuring that the guidelines laid down by the centre are adhered to.

In 1970, the Labour Party's national agent wrote to his regional organisers 'giving an A—Z on how it [reorganisation] should be carried out. Everywhere they go they represent the NEC.'[23] Regional organisers were given a timetable within which they were expected to work. As the NEC wanted the new parties to be established as soon as possible they had the task of galvanising constituency parties into swift action. Much of the preliminary work was started prior to the redistribution bill becoming law. In the West Midlands region, for example, the following circular was sent to constituency party secretaries in October 1970:

> You have recently had correspondence from the National Agent of the Labour Party in connection with the Redistribution of Parliamentary constituencies.
>
> Until Parliament has made a final decision about the Order bringing into being the new or altered constituencies, we cannot officially commence the procedure to set up the new Party

structure involved. We are already well under way with consultations with the present constituency organisations involved in major changes but so that all Constituency Parties know how we shall be tackling this involved subject, I set out below which areas we shall consider as major or minor changes. Those with minor changes will be asked to re-arrange their Parties in consultation with those neighbouring Parties involved. [24]

The initial meetings of the new constituency parties had to be called by the NEC. In effect, this meant that regional office did most of the work. (See Chapter 3 for details of the work.) In the words of one regional organiser, it was 'a massive job'. [25] The task of closing down old parties poses major problems for a regional organiser, particularly where large debts or assets are involved, so it is usual practice for constituency parties involved in reorganisation to decide amongst themselves how their assets should be divided up. The regional organiser then checks the balance sheets of the constituencies concerned to ensure that the distribution has been fair. Debts pose a particularly difficult problem since no new party is anxious to take them over. Regional office is concerned that all new parties begin on a sound financial footing and the regional organiser invariably attempts to persuade the NEC to write off outstanding debts.

Conservative Party area agents also provide assistance to constituency associations involved in Parliamentary redistribution. In 1970, when the Boundary Commission proposals were finally accepted by Parliament, a detailed guide was sent from Central Office to every constituency agent. This provided advice concerning the procedure to be adopted by constituency associations. As in the Labour Party, the area agent has an important role to play in closing down old parties and in establishing new associations. Central Office stipulated that all new constituency associations should be established by 31 March 1972. Given this broad directive, area agents were able to proceed at their own pace, provided that they followed the procedural instructions set out by Central Office.

By-elections

Labour Party regional organisers are responsible to the National Executive Committee for the conduct of all by-elections in their respective regions. Similarly, Conservative area agents are responsible to the Director of Organisation for the running of by-elections. In both parties, this entails spending much time in constituencies where by-elections are pending. The following examples serve to illustrate this point. The East Midlands regional organiser worked in the Wellingborough constituency from

14 November to 5 December 1960 pending the by-election on 4 December. At the Newcastle-under-Lyme by-election in October 1969, the West Midlands area agent worked in the constituency from 14–30 October, although he was not an election agent.

Transport House encourages regional organisers to act as election agents in all by-elections, except where there is a competent full-time agent in the constituency. In practice, however, organisers vary in their adherence to this advice. In the fourteen by-elections in the North-West region between 1956 and 1965 the regional organiser acted as the election agent in twelve. This contrasts with the East Midlands where the regional organiser has been far less concerned to exercise formal control. In the years 1953 to 1969 there were fourteen by-elections in the East Midlands, and the regional organiser acted as election agent in only six. On occasions, however, the Labour Party's national agent insists that the regional organiser act as election agent. This happened at the Leicester North-East by-election in 1962, although the regional organiser had already earmarked a local person for the job. However, a regional organiser has little alternative but to comply with instructions from headquarters.

Whether or not a regional organiser acts as election agent, he is still a key figure in an election campaign, since it is his duty to secure personnel for the campaign. He must also supervise the full-time agents who come to help in the constituency as well as the assistant regional organisers from other regions who are drafted in by the National Executive Committee. At the Bassetlaw by-election (31 October 1968), there was a total of 29 full-time agents and organisers working in the constituency.[26] The regional organiser determines how best to utilise this aid. When a regional organiser does not act as election agent he frequently assumes the role of canvass officer. He is then responsible for co-ordinating and directing the canvass throughout the constituency.

A regional organiser also has the responsibility of securing help from neighbouring constituencies. This is frequently a very difficult job, particularly if the constituency borders on another region. This problem was highlighted in the Wellingborough by-election held on 4 December 1969. In his report on the campaign, the East Midlands regional organiser wrote:

> I think we only had the help of two people from the Eastern Region during the campaign, and this region joins the constituency, in spite of all our efforts, and nobody came from Bedford, which is actually nearer to the constituency than any other place, apart from the Member of Parliament.[27]

Virtually all the assistance in the by-election came from other constituencies within the East Midlands region. Cross-regional exchange appears to be almost non-existent in the Labour Party.

Whether or not a regional organiser is appointed election agent for a by-election makes little difference to his actual role, as it is his task to supervise the campaign on behalf of the NEC. The amount of time taken up in dealing with by-elections varies from year to year. As each by-election involves about three weeks away from the office, a series of by-elections can, therefore, be extremely time-consuming. In addition, assistant regional organisers are seconded by the national agent's department to assist in by-elections in other regions. Taken together, regional staff spend a high proportion of their time dealing with by-election work. In the East Midlands region in 1967 there were two by-elections, and out of a total of 322 engagements in that year, the East Midlands regional organiser spent 46 at Parliamentary by-elections. The assistant regional organiser spent 118 out of 264 visits, and the woman assistant regional organiser spent 86 out of 338 visits on by-election work. This amounts to 12 per cent, 40 per cent and 25 per cent respectively of their engagements during 1967. [28]

Conservative Party area agents never formally act as election agents in Parliamentary by-elections. When there is no local constituency agent, the job is taken on by a deputy area agent. For example, in the Lincoln by-election (1 March 1973), the East Midlands deputy area agent acted as election agent. This strategy has been adopted because election agents are required to attend to a whole range of legal technicalities (such as work connected with postal ballots, nomination papers, control of expenditures) during a campaign and Central Office believes that it is misusing resources to engage an area agent in such work. This routine work is delegated to other people, thereby enabling the area agent to concentrate on directing and co-ordinating the campaign.

Local government elections

During local government elections, regional organisers concentrate on the politically important local authorities. In 1969 in the West Midlands region, for example, every major local authority except Stoke was solidly Conservative. Regional office, therefore, put in a great deal of work at Stoke prior to the 1969 local government elections The assistant regional organiser spent three months there during which time he modernised the election machinery, designed a broadsheet, held schools on party organisation and dealt with policy statements. In brief, he organised the whole campaign. In marginal areas, regional office frequently supervises preparations for the campaign. It also collates local government election results and forwards them to Transport House.

The shortage of Labour Party constituency agents means a great deal of extra work for the regional staff in local government matters. [29] In 1970, for example, Derbyshire did not have a single full-time agent and much of the routine work carried out by regional office in February and March 1970 would have been unnecessary had there been even one full-time agent in the county to co-ordinate the work. The regional office staff even had to check personally that nomination forms were filled in. Finding candidates to stand in 'hopeless' areas was also a time-consuming task, but one which had to be done if at all possible. The presence of 'stooge' candidates meant that opposition forces could not be thrown in their entirety into a nearby marginal constituency.

The production of broadsheets, particularly for county council elections, is frequently undertaken by regional office. In the North-West region during the 1964 county council elections 'a four-page pictorial leaflet, in two colours, with space for the candidate's photograph and message were produced and supplied as requested. The leaflets were heavily subsidised. ... The leaflets proved very popular and nearly 600,000 were produced and circulated.' [30] In 1970, the East Midlands regional organiser produced a county broadsheet for Nottinghamshire, which was politically the most important county in his region.

As county council by-elections attract some publicity, regional office makes an effort to help ensure a good performance. The following extract gives some indication of the seriousness with which county council by-elections can be regarded by regional organisers:

> [On 30th June 1969] I was present at a meeting of the Arnold Local Labour Party which was discussing arrangements for a Nottinghamshire County Council by-election in the Bestwood Division.

> General remarks:
> This is a seat they held from 1945 to 1967 and I am anxious that a well organised campaign is conducted, as it should be possible to regain the seat. Arrangements for the campaign were made and I have already written to County Councillors and local parties in the area, stressing the importance of helping this by-election. ... I intend to watch the development of the campaign to make sure that an effective effort is put in. [31]

Conservative Party area agents involve themselves in all local government elections, except parish council elections. They have a general supervisory role, providing a network of services and advice to candidates and local parties. The area office works with Conservative Central Office in providing assistance. The publicity department at Central Office sends out dummy election addresses, hints on publicity and similar information. Legal forms come direct from Central Office as do notes for the guidance of candidates. Despite the direct involvement of Central Office, area office plays an important role during local government elections.

As in the Labour Party, area agents must ensure that candidates are adopted in as many wards as possible. In county council elections, area agents play a supervisory and a co-ordinating role. In every county in the East Midlands Area (except Lincolnshire, where all Conservatives fought as Independents), the area staff had a series of meetings with constituency chairmen, agents and leaders of Conservative groups about policy for the 1970 election campaign. Preparations for district council elections are usually dealt with by the local constituency association agent. Counties, however, cover a large number of constituencies, and someone must get the various units together to discuss policy. By default, the task has fallen to the area agent. As in the Labour Party, effort is concentrated on the politically marginal counties. In the West Midlands, for example, the area agent has traditionally concentrated on Staffordshire, while the East Midlands area agent produces the broadsheet for Nottinghamshire, which is produced and sold from the area office.

The local government results service provided by Central Office is supplied with much of its information by area agents. Each area agent is required to collate the area's results in a prescribed manner and to transmit them to Central Office in accordance with instructions issued by the Organisation Department. Area office again mediates between the party in the county and Head Office, passing information up from the localities at the request of the leadership. Local party efforts are supervised by area staff in accordance with Head Office norms.

Conciliatory

In any political or social grouping, disputes inevitably arise from time to time. Both regional organisers and area agents arbitrate in such circumstances. In addition, regional organisers are occasionally required to represent the National Executive Committee on enquiries at the local or constituency party level. Disputes occasionally arise between local parties and party groups on the Council and may also occur between party members. In short, there are many potential sources of conflict within local parties. When trouble flares, regional staff initially act as brokers between the disputing factions. In the event of a regional organiser failing to satisfy both parties, either side in the dispute may call for an official enquiry by the Labour Party's National Executive Committee. Usually, however, informal intervention by the regional organiser is sufficient to calm troubled waters. In April 1969, the East Midlands regional organiser wrote:

> I was present (on 2.4.69) at a meeting of the Blidworth Local Party (in the Newark Constituency), where difficulties had arisen between the Local party and Labour councillors on the Southwell Rural District Council regarding an increase in Council house rents and an amendment to the agreements between tenants and the local council.
>
> It seemed to me that basically this was a dispute between the National Union of Mineworkers and the National Association of Colliery Overmen, Deputies and Shotfirers, as the meeting lined up on this basis. I think, as a result of a bit of straight talking by both the Agent and myself, the Local Party now see the matter in a different light and I am hoping the problem will be resolved. [32]

To take another example – this time from the West Midlands region – the regional organiser visited the Meriden Constituency Labour Party in November 1969.

> To meet the Constituency Party Executive Committee and the officers of the Kingshurst Local Labour Party to try to reconcile differences between the Local Party and the constituency.
>
> We had a very lengthy discussion on this long standing dispute. It goes back a few years and is really based on personal clashes with the Secretary of the Local Labour Party.
>
> I hope we cleared the air and that the Local Party and the Constituency Party will find it possible to co-operate in a much better spirit in the future.
>
> The minor points which cause the arguments are enlarged because of the very considerable problems both the Constituency and the Local Party have to face in this rapidly expanding constituency where a new population of over 50,000 people will be created within three years. [33]

Occasionally, however, regional organisers are unable to reach a satisfactory settlement. An appeal by one of the dissenting parties to the National Executive Committee obligates the NEC to set up a formal enquiry to examine the problem. In most instances, Head Office will ask the regional council to conduct the enquiry, particularly if the matter is a purely local issue (such as a party member being expelled by the local constituency party). The regional organiser must arrange the hearing and take the minutes. He himself, however, will rarely act as one of the judges, since he will invariably have been involved in the dispute at an earlier stage. Three members of the regional council usually conduct these local enquiries, which are, in any event, few and far between. A typical regional enquiry was held on 18 February 1969 in the East Midlands into the refusal of the Mansfield Constituency Labour Party to accept a Mr J. Thierry as a member. [34] At other times, enquiries consist of a combination of regional and national representatives, and, very occasionally, an enquiry is conducted purely by national personnel. The formal position of regional organisers is, however, relatively unimportant when compared to their troubleshooting role of arbitrating in local party disputes before they reach the enquiry stage. Being an outsider, a regional organiser can often restore unity before any permanent damage is done.

Formally, Conservative Party area agents do not have an important role to play in settling disputes within the party. Their role is outlined in the rules of each area council. In the West Midlands, for example, the rules state:

> The officers of the Council shall give decisions upon or take such steps as they think fit to bring about a settlement of any dispute or difference submitted by the Executive Council of any Constituency Association or Central Council of a divided Borough (being a member of the National Union). If the officers of the Council shall fail to bring about a settlement acceptable to all parties to the dispute or difference the Executive Council of the Association or Central Association of a divided Borough may (and shall if so requested by any Branch of the Association) submit such dispute or difference to the Executive Committee of the National Union, which may give a decision thereon or take such steps as it thinks fit to bring about a settlement. Any decision given in writing under the hand of the Chairman for the time being of the Executive Committee of the National Union shall be final and conclusive. [35]

As an officer of the Council, the area agent is entitled to attend any enquiry. He usually does not attend, however, as most area agents like to appear to remain uninvolved in official disputes for diplomatic reasons. In any event, they are few and far between. The West Midlands Area provides a convenient example. At the Executive Committee meeting of the West Midlands Conservative Council, held on the 24 October 1970, the area agent reported that 'he had received a letter from Mr R.A. Millard, Chairman of the Bromsgrove Divisional Conservative Association stating that the Crabbs Cross Branch of his association had declared a dispute and he, therefore, was committing the matter to the West Midlands Area'. [36] A committee of three was appointed to deal with the matter, and the deputy area agent for the West Midlands acted as the secretary of the Committee. Formally, area agents 'have no authority to arbitrate in any disputes in the Conservative Party. We can offer advice or occasionally "bang heads" together, but the rules of the National Union clearly lay down who may arbitrate in disputes.'[37] As in the Labour Party, however, formal enquiries are the exception rather than the rule. Informal work helps to ensure that the bulk of local difficulties never reach the official dispute stage. It may be something of a tribute to the informal work of the regional and area staff that there are not more public disputes within the two parties.

Advisory

Regional organisers and area agents provide advice on organisational and policy matters. Not surprisingly, poorly organised constituencies make the most use of their expertise. The need for help is far less pressing in constituencies where there is a full-time agent or where there is a large pool of voluntary help to call upon. Nevertheless, it would be incorrect to say that in the Labour Party only poorly organised constituency parties contact regional office for advice. On occasions, particularly when there is a dispute in a constituency, regional advice will be sought by the safest constituencies. The range of matters upon which advice is sought is immense, although questions about local government tend to predominate. The following series of examples, taken from the East Midlands region, indicates the type of enquiries with which regional organisers deal.

On 5 November 1969, the regional organiser had an interview with the chairman of Melton constituency Labour Party. In his report to Head Office the regional organiser wrote:

> The Chairman was concerned about a report which was being presented by a sub-committee the Constituency Party had established to review organisation. He had let me see a copy of the report and I told him that there were a number of suggestions in it which conflicted with the Party Constitution and he could not, therefore, put them into practice. I have since written to the Constituency Party Chairman and am now awaiting the outcome of the meeting where the matter was discussed. [38]

71

Earlier in the year, the regional organiser had visited Holland-with-Boston 'to interview the newly appointed election agent for this constituency . . . who will be running an election for the first time, and the object of this visit was to discuss all the details involved. I let him have a copy of *Conduct of Parliamentary Elections* and also gave him details of a conference we shall be organising for constituencies without full-time agents.'[39]

In May 1969, the regional organiser visited Mansfield to 'meet the Secretary to discuss Local Government Elections in Mansfield and Warsop'. [40]

The final example is taken from Derby Borough Labour Party:

> I had an interview with the Secretary/Agent regarding the Party's project to enter the launderette business.
>
> I had obtained some very useful information on the financing and operation of launderettes via the Nottingham Co-operative Society, and from this it would seem to me that the proposition the Derby Party have in mind will not be viable. I am enclosing a copy of the letter I have received for your information. I am hoping, as a result of this information, the Derby Party will give up the idea. [41]

These examples indicate the range of advice which regional organisers give. In addition to formal visits, contact with constituency parties is maintained through the telephone. Specialist matters, such as the acquisition of premises for clubs and the utilisation of party property situated in town centres, are rarely dealt with at the regional level, but are usually passed on to Head Office to be dealt with by the relevant specialist. Regional advice is largely limited to matters of party organisation at the local level.

The Conservative Party has more full-time agents at the constituency level than the Labour Party. Area office is, therefore, used less frequently for advice — no doubt partly because too much reliance on the area office is felt to reveal incompetence at the constituency level. As in the Labour Party, questions about local government and electoral law constitute a large percentage of enquiries.

Regional and area organisers advise committees for the appointment of magistrates and other public boards. The North-West region of the Labour Party has a magisterial sub-committee which nominates members for consideration. To quote from its annual report, 1957:

> The Regional Council has pursued its work in this connection during the past year and parties have been circularised accordingly.

In accordance with usual practice communications were sent to all CLP's in Lancashire and Cheshire urging the submission of names through the various channels for magisterial appointment. In Lancashire appointments were satisfactory but in Cheshire appointments were not in accordance with Labour's position in the county. The Regional Executive Committee has taken appropriate action and hopes to be able to report improvement in 1957.[42]

In a letter to me, H.R. Underhill, formerly West Midlands regional organiser, now National Agent of the Labour Party, wrote: 'Most organisers are active in their capacity as Regional Council Secretaries in dealing with Magisterial appointments.'[43] Conservative Party area agents have similar influence in suggesting names for nomination, but here the process of nomination is even harder to unearth.

Servicing

Both regional organisers and area agents provide a large number of services to constituency associations, notably arranging speakers for events throughout the region and organising national, as well as regional, campaigns. In addition, regional and area staff organise and attend policy conferences at the request of Head Office, conduct schools on party organisation, and lecture at the constituency level. Publicity and press work is also important.

In the Labour Party, regional office has always provided speakers for meetings. By 1971, it had become recognised as the main channel through which constituency parties obtain speakers. Requests for speakers made directly to Head Office are referred back to the region by the Organisation Department at Transport House. The number of constituency parties which rely on their Member of Parliament using informal means to obtain speakers has been on the decline since 1970. The following extract, referring to 1949, indicates the long-standing nature of this work:

> Every effort has been made by the Regional Office to assist Parties to book speakers for Public Meetings and Party Rallies, and whilst a good number of National Speakers have addressed meetings in the Region it has been impossible to satisfy all demands.
>
> Labour MP's with constituencies in the region have readily undertaken both summer and winter propaganda meetings outside their own divisions and their services are available upon reasonable notice being given to the Regional Organiser.

In so far as it lies within the power of Head Office and the Regional Office the services of well-known speakers will be fairly allocated but Parties must not expect the impossible. Parties could make much wider use of the services of the back-bench Labour MP's for one-day Schools, Party Meetings and Public Meetings. The Regional Office is always prepared to suggest the names of other competent people for propaganda meetings and private gatherings of the Party. [44]

Requests for speakers come not only from constituency and local parties, but from a multitude of other organisations, such as trade unions, university societies, trades councils, schools and colleges. Following a reorganisation at Transport House in the late 1960s, greater responsibility over speakers was given to regional staff. Front-bench spokesmen were instructed by the Organisation Department to refuse speaking engagements which were not channelled through the Speakers' Department at Transport House. On his appointment in 1969 as National Agent of the Labour Party, Mr R.G. Hayward issued a directive to the members of his own department, stipulating that staff could not accept constituency engagements unless the relevant regional organiser had approved the visit. The informal network of friends through which some constituencies are able to obtain speakers will not, however, be easily thwarted.

In the Conservative Party, the area office is the main channel through which constituency parties and other non-political organisations obtain speakers. The extent of this task can be appreciated with reference to the West Midlands Area. During the twelve months ending June 1969, West Midlands Area Office arranged speakers for 436 meetings in the area, consisting of 47 meetings addressed by Shadow Cabinet ministers and front-bench spokesmen, 130 by back-bench Members of Parliament and 259 meetings addressed by members of the Area Panel. [45] The North-West Area likewise dealt with 188 meetings for MPs and front-bench spokesmen in the year ending April 1970, [46] besides numerous voluntary speakers on the Area Panel. Table 4.1 illustrates the numbers of speakers booked by area office in the North-West and the West Midlands.

The administrative work involved in obtaining speakers for meetings usually falls on the woman deputy area agent. As in the Labour Party, an 'old boy' network exists whereby constituencies may obtain speakers without going through the area office. Front-bench speakers are expected, however, to go via the area. An area agent will, albeit infrequently, refuse to sanction a constituency association's request for a front-bench speaker, either because the occasion is not important enough for the speaker or

Table 4.1
Speakers arranged by the area office in the
North-West and West Midlands Areas,
1965—70

	West Midlands	North-West*
1965—66	395	106
1966—67	390	86
1967—68	369	141
1968—69	436	150
1969—70	—	186

* Voluntary speakers not included. Voluntary speakers are usually people drawn from the locality, not Members of Parliament or other party notables.

because the constituency in question has exceeded its fair share of speakers. Because the demand for speakers is usually far greater than the supply, area office must try to ensure a fair allocation.

Both regional organisers and area agents are Head Office employees and, as such, adminster nationally organised campaigns. Both parties frequently hold membership campaigns, although they now occur less regularly than in the 1960s. It is usual for membership campaigns to be announced in the months following a General Election. Regional organisers in the Labour Party are given broad directives to enable flexibility from region to region. Once a membership drive has been announced the regional organiser writes to all constituency parties informing them of the campaign. The constituencies are then visited by a member of the regional staff, who explains in detail about the campaign and also sets realistic membership targets. In 1967 the Labour Party ran a membership and development campaign, which meant that the Party's regional organisers had to visit extensively. On 8 January 1969, for example, the West Midlands regional organiser visited the Leominster constituency, and observed in his report to Head Office:

This Party have accepted a target of 500 members by the end of 1967 and 750 by the end of 1968.

As the Labour vote is so small in this constituency this is a reasonable target although some members feel they may be able to do better. Membership at the moment is just over 300, but the

75

majority of these members are in the Ledbury area.

Plans were made to gradually build up Party membership and there is considerable social activity also under way. [47]

In some regions, constituencies are grouped together for the regional consultations. Writing at the outset of the national membership campaign in 1952, the East Midlands regional organiser observed:

> We have decided that the energies of the Regional Office could best be used if they were directed towards:
> 1 The marginal constituencies.
> 2 The Parties whose membership stood below 1,000 on 31st December 1951.
> We aim to visit all these Parties and discuss with them their organisation. We shall review the collecting machinery, the efficiency or otherwise of existing parties, the villages in the county constituencies where parties ought to be formed, particularly where we have contacts, and which parties are able to give help in other parts of the constituency.
> Having got all this information we shall then discuss the plans for the campaign. These plans are obviously based on the conditions found as a result of the investigation.
> The plans in the main are devised to build up the weak parties and set up the new ones. Even in the boroughs we are trying to get our people to concentrate on the weak wards. Many constituencies are running autumn campaigns built round their MP or Prospective Parliamentary Candidate, all of whom are readily responding to the requests of their constituency parties.
> We do not always get our suggestions carried out. We would think something was wrong if every party agreed with our ideas. But the individual approach is showing results. [48]

Like their Labour counterparts, Conservative area agents are involved in work resulting from national directives. Membership campaigns and the annual contracting-out campaign are the main aspects of this work. As the field agents of Central Office, they direct these national campaigns in their own area, working within a broad framework of action set down by Head Office. In 1958, for example, a national membership drive was initiated. The following quotation, taken from the minutes of the Finance and General Purposes Committee of the North-West Provincial Area indicates what this involves at the area level:

Recruiting Campaign

The Honorary Secretary gave a comprehensive report on the National Membership Campaign which is to take place in the Autumn from 16th September to 16th December.

It was agreed that a series of four group conferences should be held in the summer during the end of June or beginning of July, in order that members of the Membership Campaign Committee could attend and speak about the arrangements. [49]

Every autumn, the Conservative Party organises a national 'contracting-out' campaign, in which each constituency association is encouraged to take part. This is directed by area office on instructions from Head Office and is aimed at persuading Conservative trade unionists to opt out of paying their political levy. At this time, the area agent writes to constituency associations, enclosing sample literature and providing details of the campaign. Constituencies which fail to respond are periodically reminded by area office of their responsibilities although, in the final analysis, the area agent has no power to dictate to constituency associations.

Other national campaigns are initiated from time to time. Again, these necessitate administrative oversight by the area office. At the 1965 Party Conference the 'Ten Shilling Unit' Campaign was launched with the aim of boosting party finance. 'In the West Midlands Area, three briefing meetings were held prior to the campaign for constituency officers and agents. These were held at Birmingham, Droitwich and Wolverhampton. Nearly every Constituency in the Area participated in the Campaign, meeting with varying success. Some constituencies did very well.' [50] Likewise, the National Fund-Raising Campaign 1967/8 involved area agents. The North-West Provincial Area Annual Report for 1968 stated:

A special National Fund-Raising Campaign Committee has been set up in the Area, and, as a result, detailed plans for the campaign have been drawn up. All sections of the Party — both at constituency and Area level — will have to pull together in order to achieve our substantial Area target. [51]

Both parties, particularly when in government, arrange policy conferences 'so that the policies of the Government can be discussed with Party members'. [52] The Labour Party, for example, held a recent series of conferences entitled 'The Policies of the Labour Government'. Between January and November 1967 the North-West Regional Office organised 13 conferences. [53] In the year June 1967/8 there were 19 policy conferences in the West Midlands Region, [54] while in the East Midlands Region 14 conferences were organised. [55] The speakers for these conferences are provided by Head Office, regional office being responsible for booking halls, printing tickets, sending out credentials to delegates, arranging meals and accommodation. The initiatives for these conferences come from Transport House and the regional organiser must give effect to these initiatives locally.

The Conservative Party stages policy conferences far less frequently. The internal debates over nuclear disarmament in the 1950s and the Industrial Relations Bill in 1971 were two examples of topics which were made the subject of policy conferences. To quote from the minutes of the North-West Provincial Area Finance and General Purposes Committee, 25 April 1958:

> Nuclear Disarmament Meetings.
>
> The Hon. Sec. reported that mass meetings were being held in various parts of the country including Manchester, in connection with Nuclear Disarmament, and that the Chairman of the Party considered that every effort should be made to put forward our own point of view and to oppose the Pacifist ideas which were being promulgated. [56]

The Industrial Relations Bill of 1971 produced considerable controversy, both within the country and inside the Conservative Party. The Conservative Party leadership therefore organised a series of conferences early in 1971 to brief members on party policy. Once again, all the adminstrative details were left to the area agents. The literature sent out by area office to party leaders in the North-West in December 1971 stated: 'Leaders of the Conservative Party, at all levels of our organisation, need to be fully briefed on this important Bill.'[57]

Both regional organisers and area agents organise day and weekend conferences on their own initiative. These usually concentrate on the duties of party officers, election organisation, and similar matters. In the twelve months from May 1968 to May 1969 there were four weekend schools sponsored by the West Midlands Labour Party; three youth schools were also held. In the twelve months from March 1969 to March 1970 there were two main schools (including a one-week conference), two youth schools and four women's schools in the North-West Region. In addition, in 1969 all agents or potential agents for the forthcoming General Election were invited to attend one of three weekend residential conferences dealing with election preparations. There was also a conference for agents and city party secretaries in October 1969, bringing a total of twelve residential conferences during the twelve-month period. In the East Midlands Region there were four weekend conferences in the period from June 1973 to June 1974, one of these being a Young Socialists Conference, and one being for prospective Parliamentary candidates. [58]

Numerous one-day conferences are organised by regional offices, particularly in the period immediately prior to local government elections, at which questions of policy and organisation are dealt with by regional staff and guest speakers. Between April 1969 and March 1970 there were 41 conferences (including the four weekend schools) in the East Midlands region. Regional organisers not only organise these conferences but also frequently have to lecture as well.

In the Conservative Party, each area agent arranges his own conferences on organisation. The West Midlands Area, for example, traditionally has a series of 'Organisation Suppers' every February to discuss forthcoming local government elections. In February 1965, for instance, a series of such suppers was held 'at Droitwich, Stoke-on-Trent, Wolverhampton, Shrewsbury, Leamington Spa and Gloucester. Representatives from Constituency Associations were present to hear an address by Mr J. Galloway, OBE (the Area Agent), and to take part in discussions which were led by the Area Chairman, Mr G.M. Argles, OBE.'[59] There are, however, fewer policy conferences in the Conservative Party.

Regional and area offices provide a service to constituency associations on press and publicity matters. This service is, or course, most widely used at election times. In February 1969, following the report of the Committee of Enquiry into Party Organisation in 1968, Labour Party assistant regional organisers were given a crash course in public relations. The 1969 Labour Party Annual Conference Report stated: 'Twenty-five tutors, some professional lecturers, other highly skilled professional people in the world of communications dealt with 26 subjects and all aspects of public relations were covered.'[60] This short course was an attempt to train regional staff in the basic principles of press and publicity work, although, in practice, there are relatively few calls upon regional office to provide such a service outside election times. Although the local newspapers are quick to telephone regional office if a local story is referred to in the national press, and although regional organisers circulate the press when front-bench speakers visit the region, it is a mistake to exaggerate the importance of regional office in press matters. The national party machine plays the dominant role.

Television and radio networks often work through regional office in their dealings with constituencies, and regional organisers are occasionally asked to select a speaker on a particular topic. The advent of local radio has meant an increased volume of work, but it is still by no means heavy. Outside General Elections, regional office has a relatively minor press and publicity role.

Until 1968, each Conservative area had a full-time press officer. A streamlining of staff, however, resulted in the sacking of the press officers, along with the CPC and trade union organisers. At the 1968 Party Conference, Mr Anthony Barber, the Party Chairman, remarked that 'Relations with the press, radio and television ... are of such importance that I decided that they should be the responsibility of the Area Agent himself.'[61] In practice, however, deputy area agents now deal with press relations.

Conservative Party activists are encouraged to write letters to the press and area office co-ordinates this work. To quote the 1967 East Midlands Annual Report: 'while there has been a greater interest in writing political letters to the local Press, there is room for an improvement and help in this valuable way of getting over Conservative principles is always available from the Press Office.'[62] In the North-West the 'letters to the press' service is very highly organised:

> The Area letter-writers' panel has supplied contributors with a regular flow of material for readers' letters and this has resulted in an increased number of column inches being secured in the readers' letter columns. Considerable importance is attached to this aspect of the work and new members of the panel are constantly being sought.[63]

Each area operates a radio and television monitors' panel. Through this network, area office receives reports on party political broadcasts and also notes instances of unwarranted political bias in other programmes. Regular reports are sent by area office to the Broadcasting Department at Central Office where the material is analysed.

There is an emphasis on press and publicity work at the area level in the Conservative Party which is largely absent at the regional level in the Labour Party. In 1974, for example, one area report observed:

> Every effort has been made to keep up the excellent relations that exist between the Area and 'the media': newspapers, news agencies, and the radio and television companies. Particular emphasis has been made in attempting to make greater use of the BBC Local Radio Stations, which are now on the Medium Wave, and consequently are being listened to by a greater number of people than ever before. Some commercial wireless stations will come into existence in the

area, and it is essential that we co-operate with them from the outset.[64]

The greater awareness in the Conservative Party about what can be achieved through good press relations is patently absent in most Labour regional offices. Given the healthier state of Conservative organisation at the constituency level in 1974 (375 full-time agents, compared with 120 in the Labour Party),[65] area agents are in a better position to concentrate on broader area matters such as press and publicity. Nevertheless, despite the greater involvement of Labour Party regional organisers at the constituency level, this does not entirely excuse the apparent lack of interest in what has become an invaluable method of political communication.

Overview

Regional organisers and area agents are involved in a mass of work at the constituency level. It is important, however, to determine the division of work at the regional level and establish the amount of time allocated to each function. An analysis of staff visits in the East Midlands region during 1967 provides some indication of the distribution of work at the regional level in the Labour Party:

Table 4.2
The East Midlands Region: division of work, 1967[66]

	Number of visits
Mr J. Cattermole	
(Regional Organiser)	
Parliamentary candidates	15
Agency appointments	11
Parliamentary by-elections	46
Enquiries	6
General	197
Schools	4
County committees	5
Regional council	10
Miscellaneous	29
Total	323

Table 4.2 continued

	Number of visits
Mrs M. Long	
(Assistant)	
Regional council	3
Parliamentary by-elections	86
Parliamentary selections	1
CLP's, LLP's and wards	80
Regional Council Education Conferences	20
Staff, womens and national conferences	17
Local government elections	25
W.S. meetings and functions	29
Federation and central committees	24
Women's advisory councils	32
Regional women's events	6
Supper clubs	3
Miscellaneous	12
Total	338
Mr R.W. Simmons	
(Assistant)	
Parliamentary candidates	1
Parliamentary by-elections	118
Enquiry	1
General	85
County committees	3
Regional council	2
Miscellaneous	8
Young Socialists	46
Total	264

The assistant regional organisers spend a high proportion of their time at Parliamentary by-elections. In addition, much work is devoted to their special areas of activity. The assistant organiser responsible for youth made 46 visits in connection with youth activities, and the assistant organiser responsible for women made 94 visits to womens' sections during 1967. The assistants organise activities for their respective sections.

The distribution of work within a Conservative Party area office can be illustrated with reference to the West Midlands area in 1968:

Table 4.3
The West Midlands Area: division of work, 1968 [67]

J. Galloway (Area Agent)
Members of Parliament
Candidates
Agents
Finance
Critical seats
Publicity and press policy

Mrs Wyatt (Deputy)
Women
Speakers
Universities
National Speaking Competition

Mr Stringer (Deputy)
Local Government
Area Council matters
Internal office administration
Area office staff
Trainees
Conservative Clubs liaison

Mr Peel (Deputy)
CPC
Industrial Department (T.U.'s)
Education Department (teachers)
Publicity and press executive duties

Mr Simpson (Young Conservative Organiser)
Young Conservatives

In an accompanying note to constituency party agents, the area agent wrote:

> Liaison with Constituency Associations and sections thereof, and attendance at Constituency Association and Sectional Meetings, is the responsibility of every member of the staff.
>
> I, as Central Office Agent, have ultimate responsibility for all Departments and Deputy Central Office Agents and the Young Conservative Organiser work under my general direction. Although the various departments have been allocated as shown above, the

staff do not work in water-tight compartments and as and where and when necessary, everybody is ready and willing to weigh in to work in any department. [68]

Conclusion

Within the Conservative Party, there is a degree of functional specialisation at the area level which is largely absent in the Labour Party. Labour Party regional organisers are essentially generalists in their work, unable to specialise to any great degree because of the gaps in constituency and local party organisation. The only exceptions are the assistant regional organisers, who each concentrate on either women's or youth work. The greater professionalism of the Conservative Party's local organisation has enabled greater effort to be devoted to broader organisational matters. The usefulness of this work must be questioned. Given the poor state of Labour Party constituency organisation, regional organisers are utilised to the full in dealing with problems as they arise. The relatively healthy state of much of the Conservative Party's constituency organisation has meant less work for area agents at the grass-roots level. Indeed, in areas with a high proportion of full-time constituency agents like the West Midlands, the value of maintaining one area agent, four deputies, a press officer, a youth officer and several secretaries must be open to question. [69]

Notes

[1] A. Ranney, *Pathways to Parliament,* London 1965, pp. 3, 132.

[2] Ibid., pp. 143, 144.

[3] M.D. Rush, *The Selection of Parliamentary Candidates in the Conservative and Labour Parties,* PhD thesis, Sheffield 1965; also, *The Selection of Parliamentary Candidates,* London 1969.

[4] M.D. Rush, *The Selection of Parliamentary Candidates,* London 1969, p. 135.

[5] M.D. Rush, thesis, op.cit., pp. 453–7.

[6] See Dick Taverne, *The Future of the Left,* London 1974, Chapter 2; also 'London Diary' in *New Statesman,* 29 October 1971, p. 584.

[7] Patrick Seyd, 'The Tavernite' in *Political Quarterly,* 1974, p. 244 (author's italics).

[8] In a letter to the author (16 September 1974) Mr Jim Cattermole, the East Midlands Regional Organiser in 1962, observed: 'There are a

84

number of inaccuracies in this [review of Taverne's book by Patrick Seyd], including the number of delegates who were present at Dick Taverne's original selection conference. From my recollection, there were 63 not 43 [as Seyd stated] and in view of all the battles going on inside the Party in 1962, this was not bad.'

9 M.D. Rush, thesis, op.cit., pp. 155–6.

10 Ibid., p. 160.

11 1968 Conservative Party Annual Conference Report, p. 77.

12 Area agent, interview, 28 January 1971.

13 Area agent, interview, 16 June 1974.

14 Ibid.

15 *Liverpool Daily Post,* 28 April 1955, p. 1; 29 April, p. 7.

16 For detailed accounts of both these episodes see A. Ranney, op.cit., pp. 188–91.

17 Report to Head Office, West Midlands Regional Organiser. Reference M.365, date of visit 21 May 1969.

18 W. Burley, West Midlands Assistant Regional Organiser, interview, 1 November 1970.

19 J. Cattermole, East Midlands Regional Organiser, interview, 19 November 1970.

20 Report to Head Office, East Midlands Regional Organiser. Reference L.345, date of visit 9 December 1969.

21 The National Agency Scheme was established by the Labour Party's National Executive Committee in 1969 to try and ensure that key marginal constituencies had full-time agents for the forthcoming General Election. The party set aside £50,000 for three years to help finance agents in 43 constituencies. In September 1974 there were 41 agents within the National Agency Scheme.

22 West Midlands area agent, J. Galloway, interview, 9 December 1969.

23 R. Hayward, then National Agent of the Labour Party, interview, 11 November 1970.

24 West Midlands Regional Office. Circular to West Midlands Constituency Party Secretaries, October 1970.

25 L.R. Chamberlain, West Midlands Regional Organiser, interview, 19 January 1971.

26 East Midlands Regional Organiser, Report to Head Office on the Bassetlaw by-election. Reference: L.34.

27 East Midlands Regional Organiser, Report to Head Office on the Wellingborough by-election, 4 December 1969. Reference: L.328.

28 Figures taken from East Midlands Regional Office evidence to the Simpson Committee on Party Organisation, 1968.

[29] In September 1974, the Labour Party had only 120 full-time agents compared with 375 in the Conservative Party.

[30] 1965 North-West Regional Council Annual Report, p. 16.

[31] East Midlands Regional Organiser, Report to Head Office. Reference K.32, date 30 June 1969.

[32] East Midlands Regional Organiser, Report to Head Office. Reference L.344, date 2 April 1969.

[33] West Midlands Regional Organiser, Report to Head Office. Reference M.420, date 25 November 1969.

[34] Information from Report to Head Office by the East Midlands Regional Organiser. Reference L.343, date 18 February 1969.

[35] West Midlands Conservative Council, Rules, pp. 11, 12.

[36] Minutes of the Executive Committee of the West Midlands Area Council, 24 October 1970.

[37] E. Ward, East Midlands Deputy Central Office Area Agent, letter to the author, 13 November 1970.

[38] East Midlands Regional Organiser, Report to Head Office. Reference L.232, date 5 November 1969.

[39] East Midlands Regional Organiser, Report to Head Office. Reference K.237, date 1 August 1969.

[40] East Midlands Regional Organiser, Report to Head Office. Reference L.343, date 1 May 1969.

[41] East Midlands Regional Organiser, Report to Head Office. Reference L.50/51, date 14 October 1969.

[42] 1957 North-West Regional Council Annual Report, p. 16.

[43] H.R. Underhill, letter to author, 23 November 1970.

[44] 1949 East Midlands Regional Council Annual Report, pp. 7, 8.

[45] 1968/69 West Midlands Conservative Council Annual Report, p. 5.

[46] 1970 North-West Provincial Area Annual Report, p. 12.

[47] West Midlands Regional Organiser, Report to Head Office. Reference M.138, date 8 January 1967.

[48] *Labour Organiser* XXXI, no. 365, September 1952, p. 178.

[49] Minutes of the North-West Provincial Council Finance and General Purposes Committee, 25 April 1958.

[50] 1965/6 West Midlands Conservative Council Annual Report, p. 7.

[51] 1968 North-West Provincial Area Annual Report, p. 8.

[52] 1968 West Midlands Regional Council Annual Report, p. 4.

[53] 1968 North-West Regional Council Annual Report, p. 7.

[54] 1968 West Midlands Regional Council Annual Report, p. 4.

[55] 1968 East Midlands Regional Council Annual Report, p. 5.

[56] North-West Provincial Area Finance and General Purposes

Committee Minutes, 25 April 1958.

[57] North-Western Area Office party documents, 1971.

[58] Information from the respective regional council annual reports.

[59] 1966 West Midlands Conservative Council Annual Report, p. 8.

[60] 1969 Labour Party Annual Conference Report, p. 34.

[61] 1968 Conservative Party Annual Conference Report, p. 24.

[62] 1966/7 East Midlands Area Council Annual Report, p. 11.

[63] 1970 North-West Provincial Area Annual Report, p. 11.

[64] 1973/4 East Midlands Area Council Annual Report, p. 12.

[65] These figures refer to September 1974; information from the respective party head offices.

[66] East Midlands Regional Office. Evidence presented to the Simpson Committee on Party Organisation, 1968.

[67] Document circulated by West Midlands Area Office, 1 August 1968.

[68] Ibid.

[69] This was the establishment of the West Midlands Area Office in July 1974.

5 The Constituency/Regional Relationship: A Framework for Analysis

Both regional organisers and area agents are employed by their national party organisations, yet spend much of their time working at the constituency level. This chapter discusses some of the most important factors determining the extent of regional and area intervention at the constituency level, namely the authority/influence of regional and area staff, the professionalism of constituency party organisation and the financial position of constituency parties. It also examines the extent to which the involvement of regional and area organisers poses a threat to constituency autonomy. Inevitably there will be some overlap with previous chapters, but this will be kept to a minimum. The relationship between city parties and regional/area staff is sufficiently distinct to merit separate examination and is dealt with in Chapter 6.

Authority/influence

In both the Labour and Conservative Parties, the relationship between constituency parties and regional officials is rather uncertain. The confusion in the Labour Party was evident in 1926 when the July edition of *The Labour Organiser* carried an article under the heading 'Answers to Correspondents':

> Question:— I should be obliged if you would let me know the relationship between Labour Parties and Regional Organisers. What duties are required of these comrades and what rights have they with respect to Labour Party Organisations within their areas?

> Answer:— Some friends have a penchant for asking awkward questions and this is one. In our postal reply to this question we stated that the powers of regional officers are merely those reflected from the Head Office. Such powers as are possessed by the Party are exercised in some part through its regional officers, who also exercise

a well-understood and accepted initiative in unorganised or partly organised areas, and of co-ordination between local parties in the interests of national and regional organisation. We added that it was impossible to define in terms everything implied in that answer, and that usually good sense, tact and mutual interest solved any fine points about financial limits, and we said that these faculties have to be exercised all round to get the best results.

Our correspondent pressed us for something more definite and we replied that the functions and duties of regional officers were nowhere precisely laid down; nor for that matter were the functions of the National Executive Committee to whom they were responsible.

As the inquiry came from a constituency where an agent was employed, we added that usually the fact that an agent was employed, meant less for the Head Office officials to do. But on the other hand the fact of an agent's employment did not itself diminish any rights or functions the Head Office possessed. Rather in one sense it added to the responsibilities, for the work of supervision was just one of the functions that was fairly clear, and was implied in the grant made.[1]

All Conservative Party literature on organisation emphasises the importance of constituency autonomy. *The Final Report of the Committee on Party Organisation* (The Maxwell-Fyfe Report) stated:

The basis of the Conservative Party is the constituency association. Every association is an autonomous body. It appoints its own officers, adopts its own candidate, selects its own agent and runs its own organisation in its own way. .... In order to facilitate regular contact with constituencies and to ensure that their requirements are promptly and sympathetically dealt with, the Central Office has a branch in each of the twelve areas of England and Wales under an official known as the Central Office Agent. It should be understood that, although the Central Office keeps in close touch with the areas through the area offices, no orders can be given to the constituency associations either by the Central Office or by the area offices. The co-operation of constituencies is generally assured through personal relationships between the Association officers and the Central Office Agent.[2]

Neither Central Office nor the area agent is invested with authority at the constituency level. Area agents may advise and suggest, but they are not in a position to dictate a particular course of action to a constituency association. Area office has a servicing function for constituencies that was emphasised as early as 1907 by J.G. Shaw, the first Secretary of the Midland Union of Conservative Associations. In a circular, dated May 1907, Shaw wrote:

> It should, at the outset, be clearly understood that the Midland Union does not in any way attempt to interfere with, or take part in, the work of the party in any constituency, unless it receives a specific request to do so. The Midland Union is intended to be, and is, a conservative body, and should be regarded as a parent association, to which the leading Conservatives in the Midlands may, at all times, turn for advice and assistance.[3]

The emphasis on advice and assistance was taken up by the Maxwell-Fyfe Committee: 'The role of the Central Office is to guide, inspire and co-ordinate the work of the party throughout the country, to advise and assist constituency associations and area councils and to provide such services as can best be organised centrally.' The Conservative Party's organisational handbook also stresses the provision of services for constituency associations:

> It is the duty of these [area] officials to transact Central Office business in the area, and to act as a channel of communication between the Central Office, the area and the constituencies. They are available to help and advise the various party organisations in the area, and should be invited to attend in an advisory capacity meetings of associations and executives.[5]

This emphasis on the provision of advice and services is fundamental to the constituency/area relationship. As in the Labour Party, it is incorrect to talk in terms of 'authority'. Area agents have little authority at the constituency level although, like Labour Party regional organisers, they may have 'influence', particularly where the local unit is organisationally weak. One area agent summarised the position as follows: 'The area agent has no authority except in his own office. The constituencies are not subject to his authority in the strictest sense of the word. Such authority as he has is moral authority. He is in no position to instruct anybody. He cannot give an order to any constituency agent.'[6] Another area agent also recognised that he had 'very little formal power. The relationship is almost entirely one of contact and influence. They [the constituency associations] make the contacts and you can use the influence.'[7]

This lack of authority over constituency associations characterises all levels of the Central Office hierarchy. In his memoirs Lord Woolton wrote:

> I faced up to the fact that whilst as Chairman of the Party I had received an enthusiastic welcome from the associations, I had, on paper, no control over their activities: they selected their candidates; they selected their agent, and employed him; they arranged their meetings, and were at liberty to make direct approach to any speaker they desired. I depended on their good will, which obviously they were anxious to give, in the creation of a headquarters staff which would be so efficient in performance and so approachable in manner that their influence would overcome their lack of authority.[8]

Constituency party autonomy is more than an abstract concept. In 1963, the Stratford-on-Avon constituency agent refused to allow any Central Office representative to assist in the Parliamentary by-election. The area agent was absent at the time so Central Office sent a replacement from London who, on his arrival, was promptly told to leave by the constituency agent. Again, in 1969, the Smethwick constituency selected its prospective Parliamentary candidate without inviting the area agent to attend the selection conference. In the Labour Party, such a selection would have been invalid, but, in the Conservative Party, it was not necessary before March 1972 for a representative of Head Office to be present at selection conferences.

Traditionally, there have been important differences between the two parties in their constituency/regional relationships. The NEC must be represented at all prospective Parliamentary candidate selection conferences, and there are similar powers over the selection of constituency agents. In effect, these requirements mean that unless a regional organiser or one of his assistants attends such meetings they are invalid. It was not until March 1972, when the Central Council approved the interim report of the Review Committee on the Selection and Adoption of Candidates,[9] that the Conservative Party regularised the position of area agents at candidate selection conferences. Now 'the Central Office Area Agent, or a Deputy, should be invited to attend all meetings of the [Constituency Selection] Committee in an advisory capacity'.[10] Previously, such invitations were optional.

The establishment in 1969 of the Labour Party's National Agency Scheme endowed regional organisers with some authority in those constituencies employing an agent from the service (41 out of the 120 Labour Party agents were employed in the scheme in September 1974). Regional organisers can issue detailed instructions to these agents, since they are usually in the pay of the National Executive Committee. Each regional organiser must submit a quarterly report to Transport House, detailing the work to be carried out by National Agency Scheme employees, and agents who refuse to obey regional directives risk being dismissed.

In 1973 the Conservative Party introduced a scheme for the central employment of agents. This scheme, discussed more fully in the Conclusion, came into force on 1 January 1974 when 60 agents, mainly in the marginal seats, became Central Party employees. By September 1974, numbers had risen to 103, which fell below the target of 131 agents to be included in central employment by August 1974. [11] In theory at least, the Conservative Party's introduction of central employment of agents promises to provide greater leverage for area staff at the constituency level, although early indications have shown little sign of real change apart from the regular arrival of their monthly pay cheques. [12]

In both parties, respect for an organiser is a key factor in determining constituency/regional relationships. At the same time, however, respect is difficult to evaluate. Regional organisers, not unnaturally, tend to exaggerate the importance of this factor in accounting for the relationship between themselves and the constituencies. H.R. Underhill, National Agent of the Labour Party and formerly West Midlands Regional Organiser, has expressed a balanced viewpoint: 'The regional organiser does not have to be loved by everyone, but he needs to be respected, and the agents must not hesitate before they call on him in any matter.' [13]

Constituency organisation

The services provided by Labour Party regional offices are regularly sought by many constituency parties. The chronic shortage of agents in the Labour Party (only 120 in 1974) has resulted in regional staff dealing with what are often routine tasks at the constituency level. This situation contrasts with that in the Conservative Party, which employed 375 full-time constituency agents in 1974. In the Conservative Party, only the relatively few poorly organised constituencies depend on the advice and services of area office. One typical safe Conservative constituency found that the primary use of area office was 'for openers for Women's Branch bazaars'. [14] In 1970 the Conservative Party's Director of Organisation saw 'no reason why a really good constituency should trouble the area'. Recalling his period as area agent in the North-West, the Director observed that he 'had an understanding with the good constituencies to only visit once a year', [15] although extra visits would obviously be made should problems arise. The current area agent in the North-West likewise asserted: 'As regards constituencies, you do get more contact with some than others. It largely depends upon the degree of organisation at the local level. Where there is a good agent and good organisation the contact can be quite small. In tough seats with very few workers and weak organisation there is a need which area office can fill.'[16]

In 1964, Ian Trethowan summarised the position of area office as follows:

> The rather ambivalent role of these area offices reflects the position of the Central Office itself; they have no power at all over the constituency associations, who can completely ignore them, and quite often do, although for varying reasons. Other associations are on perfectly good terms with the area office, but find little reason to consult it. A well run association, with a good, experienced agent, lively officers, and a big enough income to support itself, is almost completely self-sufficient, unless it runs into some really major problem, in which case as often as not, the agent will by-pass the area office and get straight through to Smith Square.
>
> The area office comes into its own where there is a weak constituency association, probably in some Labour stronghold. The stronger associations subscribe to a fund, administered by Central Office, out of which the weaker ones can be subsidised. Although nominally Central Office still has no control over the associations, the man who pays the piper is at least well placed to 'advise' the tune. [17]

Finance

The third factor requiring examination is the financial relationship between constituency parties and regional/area units. In this context two questions must be considered. How much money is given by the centre (via area and regional offices) to help finance constituency parties? Do the parties receiving aid come more readily under the influence of the centre? Chapter 9 of Richard Rose's book, *The Problem of Party Government,* provides an excellent analysis of finance in the Labour and Conservative Parties, and readers are directed to this. [18]

In the Labour Party, most of the money which is spent locally is raised locally, although the recent introduction of the National Agency Scheme has left some constituency parties heavily dependent on central finance. During the years 1967–69, constituency Labour Parties contributed more to the National Executive Committee in the form of affiliation fees than they received from the centre in the form of grants. In 1969, for example, constituency Labour parties received £23,659, while they contributed £33,729 to NEC funds. [19]

In the Conservative Party, as Michael Pinto-Duschinsky has demonstrated, national and constituency party finances are almost entirely independent:

> The bulk of monies raised by Central Office are spent centrally and monies collected locally are spent locally. Second, insofar as there is any transfer of funds between Central Office and constituency associations, the sums coming to the centre (mostly from associations in safe constituencies) are much larger than the grants from the centre to the constituencies (the large majority of these go to associations in hopeless seats). Central Office thus depends on the constituencies. The financial self-sufficiency of the local associations together with the personal independence of the party workers greatly reduces the ability of Central Office to impose its will. [20]

Pinto-Duschinsky has shown that, in the period 1966–70, constituency associations raised some £9,750,000. This works out to an average of £4,000 per constituency per year. Grants from Central Office totalled £150,000 over the four-year period – less than £40,000 a year. [21] As Richard Rose has observed: 'In the transfer of payments between Central Office and the constituencies, the former is in the debt of the latter, for constituency quota payments in the period averaged £380,000 annually, nearly one-quarter of Central Office funds, and a little less than one-sixth of constituency funds.' [22]

Using the same figures as Pinto-Duschinsky, one could argue exactly the opposite, namely that instead of showing the strength of constituency associations, the figures indicate the strength of Central Office, which is able to appropriate more money from constituencies than it is obliged to pay back. The figures can, therefore, be interpreted in different ways. In any event, finance is an awkward variable to analyse, and the statistics provided by Pinto-Duschinsky are, of course, overall figures. To prove that constituencies in receipt of aid from the centre are more easily controlled or influenced by the area agent than those without financial help would necessitate detailed research on a single constituency basis. Constituencies receiving aid would have to be compared with those not in receipt of aid. Even then, the discovery of greater centralisation in aided constituencies is no guarantee that finance is the key variable determining the role of the area agent in these constituencies. There is no available research to substantiate the hypothesis that the degree of intervention by area office in a constituency is in direct proportion to the financial subsidies made by Central Office. When a financial grant is provided to a constituency association, however, an area agent has an influential voice in determining its size. This task, however, has declined in importance since the number of constituencies in receipt of Central Office aid has decreased markedly. In the North-Western area for example, the balance sheets emphasised not only that relatively little money was paid through area office to constituency associations, but that the total amounts have declined significantly between 1964 and 1970. Contributions to constituency agents' salaries declined from £8,998 to £1,725, contributions to clerks' salaries from £1,207 to £12. (See Table 5.1.)

Table 5.1

The Conservative Party: the North-Western area
Financial grants paid through area office to constituency
associations in the area, 1964–70[23]

Year	Contributions towards constituency agents' salaries			Contributions towards constituency clerks' salaries		
	£	s	d	£	s	d
1964	8998	9	5	1207	4	0
1965	5450	13	11	1207	4	0
1966	3888	11	7	731	13	4
1967	1548	12	11	66	1	6
19 months ending 31 March 1968	2055	6	0	47	6	6
Year ending 31 March 1970	1725	0	0	12	1	6

Detailed figures from the North-West and the West Midlands areas indicate both the size of grants made to constituency associations and also the type of constituencies receiving this aid, which was usually given specifically for the purpose of strengthening local organisation.

Table 5.2
The Conservative Party: the North-Western area
Area grants paid to constituency associations,
July—September 1958[24]

	£	s	d
Accrington	37	10	0
Bolton	16	13	4
Rochdale	8	6	8
Heywood and Royton	28	18	4
Bootle	27	1	8
Total	118	10	0

Again, between 15 September and 15 October 1967, the following grants were paid to constituencies:

Table 5.3
The Conservative Party: the North-Western area
Area grants paid to constituency associations,
15 September—15 October 1967 [25]

	£	s	d
Farnworth	25	0	0
Leigh	25	0	0
Heywood and Royton	66	13	4
Widnes	33	6	8
Preston	66	13	4
Oldham West	23	8	9
Total	240	2	1

In the year February 1955 to February 1956, the grants given in the West Midlands area were as shown in Table 5.4.

The sums given to individual constituencies are not large. In themselves, they are unlikely to be sufficient to enable an area agent to 'control' a constituency association. The weak financial state of most constituencies in receipt of aid makes them more dependent upon area office than safe Conservative constituencies, but financial aid in itself is not necessarily the sole criterion for 'control' or even 'influence' at the constituency level. It is only one of several factors which help to shape the constituency regional relationship.

Table 5.4
The Conservative Party: the West Midlands area
Area grants paid to constituency associations,
February 1955–February 1956[26]

	£	
Stoke Central	50	Local government election expenses
Meriden	500	Special remuneration
Walsall and North	500	grants
Dudley and Stourbridge	55	
West Gloucestershire	100	
Newcastle-under-Lyme	150	Missioners
South Gloucestershire	100	
Walsall South	75+50	
Rowley Regis and Tipton	150	
Stoke South	100	
Gloucester	300	

Notes

[1] *The Labour Organiser,* no. 65, July 1926, p. 10.

[2] *The Final Report of the Committee on Party Organisation* (The Maxwell-Fyfe Report), The National Union, London 1949, pp. 6, 8.

[3] From the archives of the Midland Union of Conservative Associations (held at the offices of the West Midlands Conservative Council).

[4] Maxwell-Fyfe, op.cit., p. 9.

[5] *The Party Organisation,* Conservative Central Office, London, August 1964.

[6] J. Galloway, West Midlands Area Agent, interview, 19 November 1969.

[7] A.S. Garner, North-West Area Agent, interview, 25 November 1969.

[8] *The Memoirs of the Rt.Hon. The Earl of Woolton,* London 1959, p. 333.

[9] The Review Committee into Party Organisation (The Chelmer Committee) was established by the Executive Committee of the National Union on 23 July 1970. Its terms of reference were: 'To carry out an investigation into the extent, if any, to which the Conservative Party in all its aspects outside Parliament might be made more democratic.' The Final Report of this Committee, chaired by Lord Chelmer, was published in

September 1972 but an interim report on the procedure for the selection and adoption of candidates was submitted to the Executive Committee and ultimately approved by the Central Council at Bournemouth on 24 March 1972.

[10] *Final Report of the Review Committee,* London 1972, Appendix D, p. 32.

[11] Conservative Party Director of Organisation, Sir Richard Webster, letter to author, 10 September 1974.

[12] See D. Butler and D. Kavanagh, *The British General Election of February 1974,* London 1974, pp. 202, 203.

[13] H.R. Underhill, interview, 21 January 1970.

[14] Miss J. Godfrey, agent Warwick and Leamington Constituency Association, interview, 21 May 1970.

[15] Sir Richard Webster, interview, 11 March 1970.

[16] A.S. Garner, interview, 25 November 1969.

[17] I. Trethowan, 'The Tory Strategists', *New Society,* 21 May 1964, pp. 13–15.

[18] R. Rose, *The Problem of Party Government,* London 1974, pp. 218–47.

[19] Information from 1969 Labour Party Annual Conference Report.

[20] M. Pinto-Duschinsky, 'Central Office and "Power" in the Conservative Party,' *Political Studies,* XX, no. 1, March 1972, pp. 1–16.

[21] Ibid., p. 8.

[22] R. Rose, op.cit., p. 225.

[23] Information obtained from North-West Provincial Area Annual Reports, 1965–71.

[24] Information obtained from North-West Provincial Area, Finance and General Purposes Committee Minutes, 1958.

[25] Ibid., 1967.

[26] Information obtained from West Midlands Conservative Council Finance and General Purposes Committee Reports, 1955/6.

6 The City/Regional Relationship

Introduction

City parties are sufficiently distinct from constituency parties to merit separate examination. Resistance to control by area/regional staff has nowhere been more vigorous than in the major provincial cities. Internally, city parties have tended to be exceptionally centralised and have made little use of voluntary help. While city machines argue that their centralised structure has enabled them to maintain a professional service in areas where it would otherwise be very difficult to provide a permanent organisation, regional and area organisers have maintained that centralisation has produced organisational inefficiency and inactivity. Repeated requests for a change in emphasis at the city party level have tended to antagonise city personnel. Accusations of financial and organisational inefficiency, coupled with tensions between city chief agents and regional/area staff, have often produced deep and lasting conflicts between these two organisational levels. In recent years, however, both Transport House and Central Office have largely succeeded in integrating the city parties into their regional/area organisation.

Traditionally, Conservative Party city associations have been particularly firmly opposed to integration with the area structure, and in 1974 there still remained pockets of resistance – notably Manchester. However, with the assimilation of Birmingham City Conservative Association into the West Midlands Provincial Area in July 1974 the writing was clearly on the wall for the city machines. Birmingham, the largest city in England outside London, had in 1967/8 refused to amalgamate its professional organisation with that of the West Midlands Area; in 1974, however, its only real alternative was total extinction.

This chapter examines the relationship between the city machines and the respective regional/area organisations in three of Britain's largest cities, Birmingham, Manchester and Liverpool. It also outlines the organisational pattern in a much smaller city, Leicester. The wealth upon which the strength of the Conservative Party's city machines was based began to dry up in the 1960s, and this decline in local income enabled Central Office to step in and provide some organisational direction. In the Labour Party, most city machines were fighting for survival in 1970. Manchester and

Liverpool each employed only one secretary/organiser, while Birmingham employed two, both of whom were dismissed in April 1971 for reasons of economy. During the years 1970–74 city Labour parties have tended to become increasingly dependent on services provided by regional offices. The resistance of the Conservative city associations to integration has been far more determined than that of Labour city parties. In consequence, Central Office's success in the early 1970s in integrating most city associations into its area organisation marked the end of an entire era. [1]

The degree of co-operation between Conservative city parties and area offices (the provincial arms of Central Office) has traditionally been minimal. In a report following his enquiry into party organisation in 1963, Selwyn Lloyd observed that in the Conservative Party:

> The relationship between large cities and the area within which they are situated frequently has not been a very happy one. The city organisation has tended to regard itself as something apart and able to dispense with the help which area headquarters can give. There has been the feeling that the city organisation is the independent 'empire' of the local Conservative leader or party and so unwilling to co-operate. . . . From every point of view it is desirable that the larger cities should be brought into closer co-operation with the Area and National Executive. [2]

Some years later, in 1967, Ian Trethowan argued that the city parties were 'in effect, autonomous satrapies. They act as overlords to the individual constituency organisations within the cities. They are largely independent of both Central Office and the provincial area, both in organisation and money.' [3] This was probably an accurate picture of city machines in the mid-1960s, but the position is now very different. By July 1974, integration of the large city associations into the Conservative Party's area organisation was virtually complete.

Birmingham

The Conservative Party

The post-war decline in Conservative city parties is most vividly illustrated with reference to Birmingham. H.G. Nicholas, quoting from the 1949 *Birmingham Unionist Association Yearbook*, describes the extensive nature of the city machine at the time of the 1950 General Election:

> The senior official of the organisation is the Chief Agent. Administrative and financial matters are dealt with by the Secretary.

The very extensive Women's Organisation is under the supervision of a Women's Organiser, while the Young Unionist movement also has its own organiser. There is a publicity officer responsible for press and relations work. . . . The important work of political education is in the hands of a political education officer. Special organisational matters are dealt with by the organisation officer. Each of the 13 Birmingham divisions has its own full-time certificated agent with secretarial assistance. Similarly all but two of the 38 wards has its organiser, generally certificated; they work under the divisional agents. At a similar level there are 30 or more full-time 'missioners' or paid canvassers and subscription collectors.[4]

While it retained such an elaborate organisation of its own Birmingham City Conservative Association had little contact with the West Midlands Area Office. The wealthy city party, unlike financially poor constituency units, was not reliant on area office services. Birmingham acted as an autonomous unit and regarded itself as sufficiently important to merit direct access to the centre, whether or not Central Office approved.

Birmingham agreed to accept help from the centre only when it became unable to handle its own affairs. In the 1966 General Election, for example, three marginal constituencies in Birmingham were supplied for the first time with broadsheets produced by area office. Similarly, in city by-elections, Birmingham had traditionally used its own agents, but when the number of full-time agents was reduced for financial reasons, the city association began, in the late 1960s, to use agents supplied from outside the city. Until 1966, if a Birmingham constituency ever needed outside help the city party met all expenses. The Ladywood by-election in 1969 marked something of a change. Three agents from outside the city helped in the by-election and, for the first time, Central Office met their expenses. Nevertheless, in 1970, Birmingham still prided itself on its organisational independence. As one city party official commented:

It would not really matter if there was no area office, because we are self-sufficient. For matters like speakers we go via the proper channel, which is the area, although we don't always do this. We sometimes go direct to Central Office. Without belittling the importance of the area, it would not make much odds to Birmingham if it did not exist.[5]

The relationship between city and area changed as the financial situation of the Birmingham association declined steadily during the 1950s and the 1960s. The tremendous organisational structure which characterised the city in 1949, when there was a staff of about 100, has given way to a rather weak machine which, in early 1974, employed only a chief agent and five constituency party agents to cover twelve constituencies. It is frequently argued that the root cause of the decline in Birmingham and in other cities has been the process of industrial amalgamations which has taken place in recent years. It is explained that the numerous small local industrial firms, which traditionally were the mainstay of city party finances, have either been swallowed up by national concerns or else have amalgamated with other local firms. These larger industrial units, it is claimed, contribute to party funds at the national rather than the local level — that is, if they contribute at all. Certainly, although there can be no doubt that, from the early 1960s, money has been more difficult to obtain, it is questionable to place the blame for the financial weakness of city parties solely on industrial amalgamations. Another reason often given is that city parties are organisationally top-heavy and rather inefficient, and a great deal of wealth within the cities still remains untapped. City parties, unlike constituency associations, appear to rely too much on business contributions and not enough on other methods of fund-raising. Although the precise financial position of our city parties remains a closely guarded secret, one point is clear: the wealth of city parties has declined whether through business amalgamations or for some other reason and these financial difficulties have eroded the traditional organisational independence of the large city machines. By 1970, Liverpool and Bristol were obliged to accept Central Office aid. In autumn 1971 and spring 1973 Bradford and Sheffield respectively followed suit. In 1974, Birmingham likewise accepted aid despite its earlier determination to resist all incursions by the centre.

The Labour Party

In 1948, H.R. Underhill was appointed West Midlands Regional Organiser of the Labour Party against competition from Harold Nash, Secretary of the Birmingham Borough Labour Party, who also applied for the job. There was, however, little conflict between region and city as a result of Nash's defeat, largely because regional office never attempted to dictate to the city party.

Writing of the Birmingham Labour Party in 1964, Anthony Howard observed:

> Here, if anywhere, there exists a totally centralised machine — very largely the creation of one of the party's finest organisers, Harold

Nash, who until his death earlier this year had in effect been Birmingham's Borough Labour Party. Nash had none of the professional caution of most of Labour's paid officials, he made no pretence of neutrality and frequently descended from the umpire's box into the arena to make sure that control of a constituency or the award of a parliamentary nomination went the way he had already decided it ought to go.[6]

The Birmingham organisation had likewise been praised by the Wilson Report on Party Organisation in 1955: 'We must record our view that in general (Birmingham being the one exception), the stress on city parties had led to a progressive withering away of the CLP's. In general our efficiency as a machine for fighting parliamentary elections is sacrificed to municipal considerations.'[7] Despite the optimism of the Wilson Report, constituency Labour parties in Birmingham were rapidly becoming nonentities. The highly centralised machine, with all five organisational assistants employed by the city party, was sapping the constituency parties of their activists. The centralised machine, which Nash developed, was financially successful but organisationally suspect. Although regional office recognised the dangers of excessive centralisation, once again there was 'no bossing'[8] by the region.

Nevertheless, tension was never far below the surface. An exchange in the pages of the *Labour Organiser* in 1959 provides an insight into the underlying city/region relationship. The whole affair centred around whether the city or the region should take the credit for the collection of postal votes in Birmingham during the 1959 General Election. In the October–November edition of the *Labour Organiser,* Underhill asserted that regional office had secured nearly 1,000 votes for Birmingham constituencies. This assertion provoked a reply from one of the borough party members, Mrs Joan Tomlinson. She wrote: 'Mr. Underhill's article in the November issue of the *Labour Organiser* gives the impression that the only work done in securing postal votes in Birmingham was that undertaken by the regional office. This is not so. The Birmingham Borough Labour Party had myself working as the Postal Vote Officer for four months prior to the General Election.'[9]

Underhill had the last word. In a reply to Mrs Tomlinson he wrote:

My notes did not deal with postal work done in Birmingham, but in view of Mrs Tomlinson's comments, I must now do so. From the regional office canvassing we passed to the Borough party nearly 1,000 RPF 8's for Birmingham constituencies. . . .

It is interesting to note that the total postal vote in Birmingham was 7,760, an increase of 1,754 compared with 1955. After subtracting the postal votes secured as a result of regional office activity there are only 453 additional postal votes for the whole of Birmingham. . . . It is clear that generally the Birmingham constituency parties did not achieve much success in securing additional RPF's. [10]

Such disputes typify the relationships at this level of party organisation. The borough party regarded Underhill's article as a slight on its own organising ability and, as such, it needed a reply.

The Nash era in Birmingham ended when Nash died shortly before the 1964 General Election. L.R. Chamberlain, Assistant Regional Organiser in the West Midlands, was left to oversee the campaign in Birmingham. According to Chamberlain, this undoubtedly 'helped to reduce earlier suspicion' [11] between city and region. The ARO was even given a presentation by the grateful city party after the election.

Following Nash's death, the party's finances deteriorated and the number of full-time employees decreased. The party could no longer afford the relatively large staff which had characterised the Nash regime. It was in this situation that regional office assumed a new significance. With the borough party increasingly unable to stand on its own feet, the region began to dominate a whole range of organisational matters which had traditionally been the province of the borough party. There remained, however, a certain local pride. In 1970, the borough party secretary, while admitting some contact with the regional office, was eager to assert that he would be very concerned if they 'pushed their noses into municipal affairs'. [12] Thus, in that year, Birmingham Borough Labour Party was clinging desperately to its last grain of independence, as can be seen during the redistribution of Parliamentary constituencies in 1970/1.

Late in 1970, the NEC instructed regional organisers to close down old, and to set up new, constituency parties, following the reorganisation of constituency boundaries. Regional organisers acted as NEC representatives in this task. In Birmingham, the borough party resented regional office going over its head to convene meetings in constituencies within the city. Eventually, a compromise was reached whereby regional office called the meetings but the accompanying clerical work was done by the borough party, which used its own notepaper in all communications. This compromise salvaged borough party pride.

If a city party is to resist regional encroachment, it needs financial strength in order to provide essential services for its member constituencies. In the early 1950s, Birmingham Borough Labour Party had some

£30,000 in the bank, but this was not invested and consequently disappeared over the years. By 1970, the party's annual income had dropped to £7,800. At this time, the party employed one organiser secretary, one assistant organiser and two clerks. To function at all efficiently, the party needed an annual income of some £10,000 per year. The annual deficit was, therefore, about £2,200.[13] The extent of the borough party's financial crisis was revealed at the annual meeting on 14 April 1971, when the party decided to dismiss its two organisers and one clerk for financial reasons. The annual saving was estimated at £4,700. The *Birmingham Post* reported: 'Although the party's annual financial report will show that last year's deficit is not very large, it is the future that looks black.'[14]

The 1971 crisis meant that regional office virtually assumed control in the city. With a staff of only one clerk, the borough party became reliant on the region in even routine organisational matters. The *Birmingham Post* reported on 16 April 1971 that 'the West Midlands Region of the Labour Party is preparing to give more assistance in running the movement's affairs within the city'.[15] The financial strength of the borough party in the 1950s had provided the city with a power-base in its relationship with the region. During the 1960s the borough party and regional office lived somewhat uneasily side by side. However, because it had become financially poor and organisationally weak by the early 1970s, Birmingham Borough Labour Party has, through force of circumstances, become increasingly dependent upon regional office.

Manchester

The Conservative Party

In Manchester, the friction still existing between city and area stems largely from the presence of the North-Western Area Office in the city centre. As one city party official lamented:

> Efficiency and organisation is what concerns me. With two offices in Manchester you must overlap. Voluntary workers and some professionals don't know the difference between the area and the city association office. The press particularly tend to get muddled and ring area office for something about Manchester. Sometimes the area is caught off its guard and it issues press statements which contradict, innocently, a decision already taken by the city party.[16]

The city association believes that the area is undermining its power. In such conditions distrust, and even open hostility, have flourished.

Too often, lines are crossed and, as a result, effort is duplicated. In September 1959, for example, Harold Macmillan opened the Conservative election campaign from Belle Vue in Manchester: 'Where most Conservatives would recall the occasion proudly, the city party remembers it with some bitterness. . . . "It cost us all of £500 and the only credit went to the area office".' [17] This incident, petty in the extreme, is indicative of city/area conflict in Manchester.

A major area/city tension in Manchester has been finance. Central Office has attempted to raise money in Manchester from sources which the city party has claimed as its own. Accusations of poaching, particularly in the 1960s when the party was struggling financially, caused great bitterness. Finance aside, petty aggravations sour city/area relations in the city. For example, the area organises meetings in Manchester which the city machine claims to know nothing about.

Formally, relations between city and area in Manchester are diplomatic. For example, one recent annual report observed:

> We wish to record our appreciation of the interest which the Area Chairman, Mr Percy Stephenson, and the Area Honorary Treasurer, Mr Charles Johnston, have shown in the city affairs during the year. We also thank Mr A.S. Garner, the North-West Area Agent, for his interest and assistance. . . . It is our wish to work as closely as possible with the officers of the North-West Area. [18]

In practice, however, despite the façade of cordiality, there is little love lost between Manchester City Conservative Association and the North-West Area Office. In reply to the question: 'Would it really matter if there were no area office in Manchester?', one leading city official said: 'It would be a tremendous improvement because it would cut out the frustrations which exist at present.' 'Would you lose anything?' 'No, Manchester would', he added, 'be more efficient without them.' [19]

The city party bureaucracy argues that its sectional committees (such as Women's, Young Conservatives and Conservative Political Centre) are poorly supported because the area structure has creamed off much of the best potential committee material. In general, the city party alleges that the presence of an area office in Manchester has sapped some of its energy. The veracity or otherwise of these allegations are in one sense immaterial. 'Creaming off' provides a pretext for resentment against the area, and it enables the shortcomings of the city party to be blamed on the area. In November 1974, Manchester was the one large city with a chief agent that had not been integrated into the area structure, and there seemed little immediate prospect of such a development. The Leeds City Association was also still running itself, but this much weaker city machine did not have a chief agent.

The Labour Party

By 1970, Manchester Borough Labour Party was in no position to challenge the region. Like Birmingham, it was financially impoverished and had become increasingly reliant upon the advice and services of regional office. Writing in 1964, Anthony Howard observed:

> Manchester today is in no way an entity; it is the empty shell of the vast conurbation that has grown out of it; and by living firmly in a nostalgic past, the political parties have paid a heavy price in terms of effectiveness and efficiency. The Conservative, Labour and Liberal parties all maintain a separate Manchester organisation but in each case the shadow of the regional office (also with its area headquarters within the city's boundaries) falls heavily over them. It is most marked perhaps in the case of the Labour Party. The Wilson Report of 1955 wasted no time in discussing Manchester in terms of the problems created for constituencies by the maintenance of a centralised city party. It did not need to, for the Manchester City Labour Party had obliged Harold Wilson by doing what at that time he was urging other city parties to do elsewhere; it had almost ceased to exist. Even today (with a net income of under £1,000 per annum – only £7 of it from the constituencies that make up the city) it is still desperately trying to redeem a backlog of debt . . . the battle has already been won by the regional office over the city organisation. [20]

During the post-war years, the city party's power steadily declined. R. Wallis, North-West Regional Organiser, 1936–66, was a critic of city party machines. He believed that responsibility for organisation in cities should reside at the constituency level. Wallis observed: 'The City Labour Party is a self-perpetuating organisation which does little. To keep its office and secretary, it is constantly concerned with making money. It makes little organisational impact.' Nevertheless, Wallis was prepared to admit that 'it does maintain contact with the City Council Labour Group and it also promotes candidates for the city council, and it deals with this side very efficiently'. [21]

Despite the dominance of regional office, there has always been some conflict between city and region. The proximity of regional office to the town hall [22] has, over the years, meant that leading city representatives tended, purely out of convenience, to use regional office rather than the city party offices for advice and information. This was resented by the city party. To quote Wallis: 'There was a bit of jealousy. The city secretary was conscious that people looked to regional office, not the city, for advice.' [23] To Wallis, this seemed perfectly natural since, he alleged with considerable justification, 'we were better equipped'. [24] As in Birmingham, the continuing financial plight of the city party played into the hands of regional office. The region has been able to provide a standard of service which is well beyond the rather limited resources of the city party. While tensions inevitably still exist in Manchester, they are relatively insignificant when compared with those in the late 1960s between regional office and the Borough Labour Party in Liverpool.

Liverpool

The Conservative Party

In Liverpool, as in both Birmingham and Manchester, it was only the severe financial difficulties of the 1960s that allowed Central Office to draw the city machine into the mainstream of party organisation. Liverpool had a long history of independence. Anthony Howard quotes Sir Ernest Stacey, Chairman of Liverpool City Conservative Association in 1964, as saying: 'What's that about Macleod? . . . Well, let me tell you something. He's had one or two bumps with me and I think you'll find he's singing a rather different tune now. . . . Blakenham? Yes, he came up here during the by-election and we saw him to the airport and put him on the plane back.' [25] Anthony Howard continued:

> Sadly, however, it is nowadays bombast without backing. The years of glory have departed for the Liverpool Conservatives and even their days of autonomy seem to be numbered. The by-election in Scotland last June (June 1964) marked perhaps the moment when the writing first became clearly visible on the wall. From the beginning the Liverpool Conservative Association, true to its historical tradition, had insisted that it alone would run the campaign and that it would brook no interference whether from party headquarters or from the regional office in Manchester. The result was a drop of 7,500 in the Conservative vote and the biggest swing to Labour (12½ per cent) of any by-election this year. Understandably there swiftly followed some pretty heavy hints in the Conservative press that on this basis Liverpool would very soon be required to mend its ways or fall into

line with standard party organisation in the rest of the country. [26]

During the 1960s, Liverpool was financially weak. The party had already been bailed out of one financial crisis in the 1950s, thanks to a loan from Central Office. It was only too willing to escape from its financial difficulties by permitting its chief agent to become a Central Office employee.

The Labour Party

'Liverpool looks on itself as a mini-region. It has no leanings to anything run from Manchester.' [27] Regional office, situated in Manchester, has been able to exert very little influence in Liverpool over the years. At best the relationship has been cool, at worst positively hostile.

From the establishment of the North-West Regional Council in 1938 until his retirement in 1966, R. Wallis was North-West Regional Organiser of the Labour Party. During this time, Liverpool's resentment of the regional organiser as a representative of Transport House was usually kept in check. Regional office interfered very little in the internal organisation of the joint Trades Council and Labour Party, and, by going out of his way to cultivate friendships in the city, Wallis helped to establish a relatively friendly relationship. Moreover, for some twenty years, Wallis frustrated the efforts of the NEC and the TUC to split the Liverpool Trades Council and Labour Party into two separate organisations. When Wallis resigned in 1966 relations between city and region began to deteriorate.

By the late 1960s the breach between region and city had opened wide and hostility was overt. Regional office wanted it made plain that Liverpool was an integral part of the North-West region. The new regional organiser appeared determined to split the joint Liverpool Trades Council and Labour Party. In so doing he was following an NEC directive to split the party. Playing an instrumental part in splitting such a popular unit hardly enhanced the standing of regional office on Merseyside. To understand the contemporary relationship between Liverpool and regional office it is necessary to outline the main points of this dispute.

In the early 1960s, the regional office of the Transport and General Workers Union requested an enquiry into Liverpool Trades Council and Labour Party, for reasons which were never made public. The outcome of the enquiry, held in 1962, was a proposal to separate the joint Trades Council and Labour Party, thereby splitting the industrial and political wings of the movement in Liverpool. Largely due to the efforts of Wallis at regional office, the decision to separate the two bodies was repeatedly

111

postponed, and the NEC did not pursue the matter because of the General Elections in 1964 and 1966. In August 1967, however, the Secretary of the Trades Council and Labour Party received a letter from Sara Barker, National Agent of the Labour Party, informing him that she and a representative of the TUC wished to meet the executive committee of the Trades Council and Labour Party in order to implement the 1962 decision.

Nothing further happened until 27 November 1968, when the national agent sent a letter informing the Secretary of the Trades Council and Labour Party that the North-West regional organiser would be attending the next meeting of the Trades Council and Labour Party, where he would outline the situation. On 13 December 1968, P. Carmody, the new regional organiser, attended the executive committee's meeting, acting for the Labour Party's NEC. He announced that, as from 31 January 1969, a new borough party would be set up. In fact, 'the new Borough Labour Party was formed on 20th February 1969'. [28] Writing in *Tribune*, Eric Heffer MP maintained: 'The feeling in Liverpool is that the real reasons behind the insistence on the separation are political. The Liverpool Party has a long history of support for left-wing views. It has always had a turbulent history and is not easily pushed around.' [29]

Whatever the real reasons for dismantling the Trades Council and Labour Party, there can be no doubt that it was forced through by the NEC against the wishes of most people in the Liverpool Labour movement. Regional office played an active role in the operation, thereby stretching city/regional relations to breaking point. The new regional organiser might have satisfied the NEC by adopting this course of action, but in the process he alienated Liverpool.

Another major cause of discontent in the late 1960s was the way in which regional office continually bypassed the city Labour Party office in its dealings with constituencies in Liverpool. There was, at this time, little or no co-operation between the region and the Labour movement in Liverpool. In the late 1960s and 1970, the regional organiser employed one of his assistants on Merseyside — but this assistant was rarely seen at city party headquarters and tended to ignore the Trades Council and Labour Party's headquarters at Transport House Liverpool in his dealings with Liverpool constituencies.

One could draw upon numerous examples to illustrate the underlying friction between Liverpool and the region during this period, but one instance will suffice. In November 1967, Simon Fraser, Secretary of the Trades Council and Labour Party, produced a booklet, *Plan for Progress*, in which he proposed a new structure for the Liverpool Labour Party. In it, Fraser maintained that the city's future lay in a highly efficient central organisation which would draw together all the talents of party members in the city and use them as a kind of 'think tank' which would feed wards and CLPs with ideas, methods and enthusiasm. [30] An accompanying proposal for the central collection of membership dues by the city party drew city and region into conflict. What annoyed Liverpool was that regional office dismissed the proposals as impractical without even visiting the city to discuss them. In a similar vein, Fraser wanted to bring together all youth organisations in Liverpool to discuss common issues. Regional office prevented him from doing this in his capacity as Secretary of the Borough Labour Party because it conflicted with the Party Constitution. Fraser therefore called these meetings in his capacity as Secretary of the Liverpool Trades Council.

Thus, by 1970, there was very little co-operation between Liverpool and regional office. Indeed, there remained a good deal of hostility, much of it stemming from the separation of the joint Trades Council and Labour Party. Traditionally, 'Liverpool has shown no great interest in the region at all'. [31] In the late 1960s, apathy turned to hostility.

Leicester

The Conservative Party

In January 1971, the city party in Leicester was replaced by a city federation, a very loose organisational structure linking Leicester's three Parliamentary constituencies. The objects of the federation are as follows:

(a) To provide an efficient organisation of the Conservative Party in the City and local authorities which form part of the Party in the City.

(b) To spread the knowledge of Conservative principles and policy and generally to promote the interests of the Party in the City and such local authorities which form part of the City for Parliamentary purposes.

(c) To secure the return of Conservative Members of Parliament for the Parliamentary Constituencies of the City of Leicester.

(d) To secure the return at local government elections of Conservative Councillors.

(e) To advise and assist the Constituency Conservative Associations in Leicester in watching the revision of the registers of electors in the interests of the Party and to take steps to ensure that all supporters who are qualified are in a position to record their votes.

(f)   To keep in touch with the Conservative Associations in neighbouring constituencies and to afford mutual assistance whenever possible.

(g)   To co-operate with the Area Council and with Party headquarters with the common aim of establishing in power a Conservative Government.

(h)   To raise adequate funds for the achievement of the foregoing objects, to provide and administer a central fund for the purpose of the City Federation and to assist the Constituency and other Conservative Associations in the City of Leicester and other local authorities which form part of the City for Parliamentary purposes. [32]

In effect the city federation does little other than employ an agent (although he joined the ranks of the centrally employed agents in August 1974). In late 1974, the party in Leicester could only afford one agent for the three constituencies although it had employed a deputy agent until 18 January 1974. [33] The federation also organises the party's weekly football draw (which made a profit of £317 in 1973/4) and the Christmas draw, which made a net profit of £345 in 1973/4 (not quite as good as the previous year). [34]

In Leicester, the three constituency associations remain the key organisational groupings and the federation with its secretary/agent is only a vague shadow of a city party. It is because of the primacy of the constituencies in Leicester that there has been little conflict with area office since, by devising a structure which plays down the importance of the city federation and concentrates effort at the constituency level, Leicester Conservatives have adopted Central Office priorities.

Leicester's financial position meant that the maintenance of a powerful city party ceased to be a reasonable possibility. In 1971, the year in which the Leicester Conservative Federation was established, revenue expenditure exceeded income by £568 on a turnover of £11,033. The pattern is not an unfamiliar one for similar city federations and city associations. In Leicester, there has been a marked drop in the number of industrial firms contributing to Conservative Party funds. In February 1974, for example, the federation agent circulated an election appeal round 700 local firms but received only 100 replies. As the agent observed: 'In the 1950s we received £10,000 from election appeals, but the small city firms have been taken over by national concerns and these groups do not contribute at the local level if at all.' [35]

The 1974 Chairman's Annual Report of the Leicester Federation observed: 'We thank Mr Peter Livingston and his staff at Area Central Office for their advice and encouragement.' [36] There is in Leicester little of the acrimony which has characterised the relationship of large city associations with area office, since the city federation is clearly a means to an end – namely, returning constituency party candidates to Parliament. The constituencies, not the city federation, are the organisational focus in this city.

The Labour Party

The Wilson Report on Party Organisation (1955) came out strongly against highly centralised city parties and Leicester came in for especially harsh criticism:

> We should like to draw attention to the position of Leicester where for all practical purposes there are virtually no constituency parties in existence. The whole organisation such as it is, is at the city or ward level. . . . In practice this means that the CLP's are dormant except at election times. . . . The work of the Party is confined to wards and the City Party. Thus, as happened in 1955, when a General Election is announced, CLP machinery has to be created *de novo* and set to work. In practice the CLP organisation in the 1955 election was almost non-existent. [37]

The Leicester Labour Party, with its emphasis on local authority rather than Parliamentary elections, represented to Transport House all that was lacking in city party machinery. In the years following the Wilson Report, the regional organiser attempted to implement major organisational changes in the city, but the city party resisted the breaking-up operation very firmly indeed and it was not until 23 August 1973, with the onset of local government reorganisation, that the Leicester Borough Labour Party finally capitulated.

In place of the Leicester Borough Labour Party came traditional constituency organisation. In 1974 there was one party organiser – an employee of the National Agency Scheme – in Leicester and, although each constituency also had its own voluntary secretary, he acted as agent for all three constituency parties in the city. In the two 1974 General Elections, the city's professional organiser acted as election agent in Leicester East. By 1974, therefore, the party machine in Leicester had fallen into line with Transport House requirements: it had a constituency-based, rather than a city-wide, organisation. Each constituency party had a membership of between 300 and 500 at that time. [38]

It fell largely to the East Midlands regional organiser to push through the required organisational changes in Leicester. From the 1960s the local Labour Party rapidly became dependent on regional office services, and the fact that, in 1974, the one professional agent in Leicester was a National Agency Scheme employee has enabled regional office to retain a fairly close watch on organisation in the city. This, however, is little different from the position in any constituency which employs an agent partly financed by the centre.

The tension between city and region characterising the early post-war years had largely disappeared by 1974, although an amendment to the proposed objects for the new District Labour Parties, tabled by Leicester West constituency party at the November 1974 party conference, indicated that there was still a desire to see a strong city party as well as constituency units. The National Executive Committee put forward the following as one of the proposed objects: 'To co-ordinate constituency activities as may be required by the Constituency Labour Parties within the area, including the collection of affiliation fees and appointment of delegates by affiliated organisation for transfer to the appropriate Constituency Labour Parties.' [39] Leicester West proposed that 'as may be required by' should be replaced by 'of' and that everything after 'area' should be deleted. [40] The ghost of the old borough party still lingered on in the city as late as November 1974, but all substance had disappeared.

Central Office intervention, 1967–74

Despite the staunch opposition of city Labour parties such as Leicester to integration with the party's regional organisation, the lack of resources in the cities has allowed Transport House to complete a fairly smooth demolition job on city parties without much difficulty. The position in the Conservative Party has been very different. The large and once wealthy city associations have traditionally resisted Central Office requests for integration with the area machinery, and in 1966 Central Office began a far more intense campaign to change the balance of power in the city associations. The catalyst was the Conservative Party's defeat in the 1964 and 1966 General Elections, when the party suffered particularly heavy losses in the cities. In December 1966, the Party Chairman, Edward du Cann, set up a committee of enquiry headed by Lord Brooke of Cumnor to make proposals for improving city organisation. The members were: Lord Brooke of Cumnor, Sir Charles Burman, Mr Peter Crossman,

116

Mrs C.M. Hartland and Alderman Herbert Redfearn.

The Committee was asked 'to inquire into the functions and workings of City Associations and Constituency Associations within Cities and the relationship of both these bodies to Provincial Areas'.[41] Four main problems were outlined by the Party Chairman: the movement from the cities to the suburbs; finance; winning back local government seats; winning back Parliamentary seats. The loss of seats in the eight large cities which Brooke examined[42] was proportionately greater than over the country as a whole in both 1964 and 1966.

The Brooke Committee reported in the summer of 1967 that the city machines had become seriously run down with half the individual constituencies within the major cities having no full-time Conservative agent and that, without agents at the constituency level, the constituency associations had become moribund, tending to leave active organisation more and more to the city association and its chief agent. In consequence, Brooke found low individual membership, a shortage of workers, and too little money raised.[43] The Committee also found that relations between city associations and the area organisation were often negligible, or else were clouded by suspicion. The independence of the city associations meant, as Brooke observed, little or no contact between city and area. In the light of this situation, the Committee recommended certain structural changes in the city/area relationship, with the aim of extending Central Office influence into the cities by interlocking the cities more closely with the areas. Brooke proposed that city chief agents should become deputy Central Office area agents and be paid by Central Office instead of by the city association. The aim was to make the area the overall authority, with the city machine an important integral component.

The intransigence of the cities has prevented Central Office from large-scale collecting within the cities — a source of much national resentment since it is felt that many firms refusing to contribute locally would have agreed to contribute to national party funds. The Brooke Report emphasised that the cities should contribute more money to the party's national work. It therefore proposed that the city associations be brought under the control of the party's Central Board of Finance. In the fields of both organisation and finance, therefore, the Brooke Report recommended that Central Office should have greater influence at the city level. The proposal that Central Office should henceforth be responsible for the salaries of the chief city officers was designed to tempt the city associations to give up their independence.

The reaction of the city parties to the Brooke proposals was mixed. At that time, because Liverpool and Bristol were in financial difficulties, they had little alternative but to succumb to the financially attractive bait offered by Central Office. Their chief agents soon became deputy Central Office area agents and their salaries were paid by Central Office instead of by the city associations.

The Brooke Report received a particularly hostile reception in Manchester. At a special meeting of the Executive Council, called to consider the proposals, there was no support at all for the Brooke scheme. As one speaker at the meeting asserted, 'We don't want to have any dictation from outside.' The overriding impression was that Central Office was anxious to tap the commercial and industrial wealth of the city – a notion which the city party found repugnant. One Manchester party official was more sceptical than most about the Brooke Report: 'The excuse for setting up the Brooke Committee was that the cities did so badly in 1964. But nobody did well. . . . The conclusions of the Brooke Committee were written before they sat. Central Office and the party leadership decided what they wanted and then they set up a committee to produce the results they wanted. Nobody is naïve enough to imagine they just set up a committee to examine the problem.'[44]

A similar outright rejection of Brooke's proposals came from the Birmingham City Conservative Association. In its evidence to Brooke, the city proposed that it should be considered as an area in its own right, but this was rejected. To the Birmingham constituency chairmen, the report 'looked like a takeover bid by Central Office', or, as one agent remarked, 'It savours of nationalisation.'[45] The overt attempt to bring Birmingham closer into the Central Office orbit was resented in the city.

Yet despite their resistance, most of the large city associations have gradually succumbed. In autumn 1971, Bradford agreed to integrate its organisation with that of area office, followed by Sheffield in spring 1973. It was not, however, until July 1974 that Central Office won its most important victory. The Birmingham city association at last agreed to integrate with the West Midlands area structure. With effect from 1 July 1974 Ivor Freeman, the chief agent, ceased to be employed by the Birmingham city party. Instead of being its chief agent, he became deputy Central Office agent in the West Midlands, responsible not only for Birmingham but for all thirty-one constituencies in the West Midlands Metropolitan County. Not only has the chief agent become a Central Office employee, but the five constituency agents servicing the twelve Birmingham constituencies have also come into the Central Office orbit. With effect from July 1974, these constituency agents joined the Central Employment Scheme of Central Office.[46] Their salaries are now paid centrally not locally. The organisational independence of which

Birmingham City Conservative Association long boasted has now disappeared. The ravages of inflation have enabled Central Office to succeed where it failed some seven years earlier.

City parties received a further blow when the representation of Central Associations was abolished by the Central Council of the National Union at its meeting on 24 March 1972. City parties had hitherto enjoyed extra representation both on the Central Council and at the Annual Party Conference, but this privilege was threatened by a concerted move to reduce the national voice of the city associations. The resolution to reduce the representation of Central Associations was opposed by Bristol, Manchester, Birmingham, Coventry, Leicester and also Northampton. Although the Central Associations claimed they were not consulted, the resolution was passed by the requisite two-thirds majority. In 1973, Bristol, Manchester and Northampton attempted to change the rules and return the extra representation to the Central Associations, but they were overwhelmingly defeated. [47]

By July 1974, then, the integration of those bastions of independence – the city associations – was almost complete. To quote one leading Central Office official: 'Really only Manchester remains outside our orbit still.' [48] The provincial arms of Central Office, the area offices, have, in effect, taken over jurisdiction in the cities.

In the post-war years, therefore, both Transport House and Central Office have successfully integrated the cities into their regional and area machines. In the Labour Party, most city organisations now have agents employed not locally but by the National Agency Scheme, and this has provided some leverage for regional organisers in their dealings with city parties. Regional staff are in a position to expect co-operation from such agents. Politically, the cities are particularly strategic for the Labour Party since much of its support is derived from urban areas. The effort expended by Transport House and its regional staff in securing new organisational structures for the cities could well be considered worthwhile since it has given the centre some influence in what is a key area of support for the party. In the Conservative Party, however, the position is rather different. In the General Election of October 1974 the eight largest provincial cities returned a total of only eight Conservative Members of Parliament out of a possible fifty-one.

Notes

[1] See David J. Wilson and Michael Pinto-Duschinsky, 'Conservative

City Machines: The End of an Era', mimeographed paper, 1975. This chapter has drawn widely on material from this article as well as from Chapter 6 of the author's thesis, *Regional Organisation in the Conservative and Labour Parties,* PhD University of Warwick 1974.

[2]   *The Selwyn Lloyd Report,* Conservative Central Office, 1963, p. 9.
[3]   Ian Trethowan, *The Times,* 29 July 1967.
[4]   H.G. Nicholas, *The British General Election of 1950,* London 1951, pp. 25, 26.
[5]   Interview, 5 February 1970.
[6]   Anthony Howard, *New Statesman,* 7 August 1964, p. 170.
[7]   1955 Labour Party Annual Conference Report, p. 81.
[8]   H.R. Underhill, interview, 21 January 1970.
[9]   *Labour Organiser,* XXXVIII, no. 450, December 1959, p. 229
[10]   Ibid., p. 230.
[11]   L.R. Chamberlain, interview, 18 November 1969.
[12]   R. Knowles, interview, 1 November 1970.
[13]   Ibid.
[14]   *The Birmingham Post,* 14 April 1971, p. 14.
[15]   *The Birmingham Post,* 16 April 1971, p. 16.
[16]   A. Bowen-Gotham, Manchester Conservative Association Chief Agent, interview, 7 April 1970.
[17]   Anthony Howard, 'City Before Party', *New Statesman,* 14 August 1964, p. 202.
[18]   City of Manchester Conservative Association, Annual Report of the Central Executive Council for the year 1969.
[19]   Interview, 7 April 1970.
[20]   Anthony Howard, 'City Before Party', *New Statesman,* 14 August 1964.
[21]   R. Wallis, interview, 3 May 1970.
[22]   North-West Regional Office has now moved out of the city centre and is now situated in Salford.
[23]   R. Wallis, interview, 3 May 1970.
[24]   Ibid.
[25]   Anthony Howard, 'Cook County U.K.', *New Statesman,* 31 July 1964, p. 138.
[26]   Ibid., p. 138.
[27]   S. Fraser, Secretary of the Liverpool Trades Council and Labour Party until 1970, interview, 8 April 1970.
[28]   Liverpool Borough Labour Party Annual Report, 1969/70, p. 1.
[29]   Eric Heffer MP, *Tribune,* 24 January 1969, pp. 6, 7.
[30]   Liverpool Borough Labour Party Annual Report, 1969/70, p. 1.

[31] S. Fraser, interview, 8 April 1970.

[32] City of Leicester Conservative Federation, Rules, p. 1.

[33] See the Leicester Conservative Federation Chairman's Annual Report, 1974, p. 1.

[34] Ibid., p. 1.

[35] A. Money, interview, 29 August 1974.

[36] Leicester Conservative Federation Chairman's Annual Report, 1974, p. 2.

[37] 1955 Labour Party Annual Conference Report, p. 80.

[38] G. Parker, agent, interview, 19 August 1974.

[39] *Reorganisation of Party Structure,* Report and recommendations presented to the Labour Party Annual Conference, November 1974, p. 43.

[40] Ibid., p. 43.

[41] Taken from a circular letter from the Conservative Party Chairman to constituency chairmen, December 1966. The Brooke Committee reported in summer 1967 but its findings were never published by the party. The major written source on the Report is an article by I. Trethowan, 'Brooke's answer to Tory provincial decay', *The Times,* 29 June 1967. See also 'The Cities Enquiry' in *Conservative Agents Journal,* September 1967.

[42] Birmingham, Manchester, Liverpool, Leeds, Sheffield, Bristol, Bradford and Hull.

[43] I. Trethowan, 'Brooke's answer to Tory provincial decay', op.cit.

[44] Interview, 18 May 1970.

[45] Interview, 18 May 1970.

[46] Information contained in letter to the author from J. Galloway, West Midlands Area Agent, 12 July 1974.

[47] I am grateful to Z. Layton-Henry of the School of Politics, University of Warwick, for drawing my attention to this development.

[48] Letter to the author, 12 July 1974.

7 The Amateur/Professional Regional Relationship

This book is primarily concerned with examining the role of professional party bureaucrats at the regional and area level. In order to put this work into perspective, however, it is necessary to briefly examine the democratic structure within which organisers at this level are often obliged to operate. Writing about Conservative Party organisation, Ian Gilmour has observed:

> Like other bureaucracies, the party bureaucracy has increased its power at the expense of the elected element. Although there are a number of committees of the National Union which meet at Central Office and which advise the party on various matters, all these bodies are more consent-gaining than decision-taking institutions. Central Office in no way controls the elected leaders of the party in Parliament — indeed it has remained firmly in their grip — but it largely controls the elected part of the party organisation.[1]

The democratic structures at the intermediate level in both parties are certainly influenced, if not controlled, by the regional and area organisers. This chapter provides an analysis of democratic organisation at the regional and area level.

The democratic environment

In the Conservative Party, each provincial area has an area council with up to 1,200 members nominated by constituency associations. In the West Midlands, for example, 1,140 delegates were eligible to attend the 1970 annual meeting of the area council. In the North-West, 957 people were invited to the area council's annual meeting in 1969. In practice, however, the average attendance tends to be much lower.[2] Area council meetings are formal affairs, at which there is little participation by constituency representatives. The formal nature of these meetings can be illustrated by the East Midlands 1974 agenda.

1   President's opening remarks.
2   Apologies for absence.
3   Minutes of the Area Council General Meeting, 27 April 1973.
4   To receive the Annual Report for 1973/4.
5   Vote of thanks to the retiring officers.
6   Election of officers.
7   To receive from the Executive Committee their recommendations for Honorary Vice-Presidents.
8   To elect one representative to the National Union Central Council.
9   To elect on the recommendation of the approved Area Committees, their representatives to the National Union Central Council.
10   To confirm the election of the Chairman and one Honorary Treasurer to the National Union Executive Committee.
11   To confirm the election of the Women, Young Conservative and Trade Unionist representatives to the National Union Executive Committee.
12   To confirm the election of the three additional representatives to the National Union Executive Committee.
13   Rt Hon. Sir Geoffrey Howe, QC, MP.
14   Adoption of Standing Orders.
15   Notices of Motion.[3]

There is always a front-bench spokesman at area council annual meetings, in the same way that Labour Party regional annual meetings always include at least one representative from the NEC to put forward party policy and rally the loyal party clientele.

Labour Party regional annual meetings also deal with a wide range of business:

1   Chairman's Address.
2   Appointment of Tellers and Scrutineers.
3   Report of Regional Executive Committee.
4   Auditor's Report.
5   Statement of Accounts and Balance Sheet.
6   Appointment of Auditors (two).
7   Address by NEC representatives.
8   Resolutions and Amendments.[4]

In the Labour Party, however, there is greater opportunity for discussion by delegates. The formal business is dealt with rapidly in order to give maximum time to resolutions and amendments submitted for discussion by affiliated organisations. Each Labour Party regional annual meeting elects an executive committee to take care of the routine administrative work of the democratic regional structure. These meetings are formal occasions, consisting largely of reports from the various regional sub-committees and working parties. The following extract indicates the limited range of matters discussed at this level:

> Mr Watts reported on the meeting he had attended at Hemel Hempstead together with the Chairman and Secretary when the future of the organising region of the Northern Home Counties had been discussed.
>
> It was unanimously agreed to record appreciation of the services of Mr Frank Barrington-Ward who had represented Oxfordshire on the West Midlands Regional Executive Committee in recent years.
>
> *Reports*
> Reports were received as follows:
>
> | | |
> |---|---|
> | Trade Union and Transport | – Mr S. Watts |
> | Local Government & Planning | – Mr J. Garwell |
> | Organisation and Propaganda | – Mr M. Prendergast |
> | Young Socialists | – Mr W.V. Burley |
> | Women's Organisations | – Miss L.C. Moody |
> | Parliamentary Group | – Mr J. Horner, MP |
>
> Special thanks were accorded to Mr Horner MP, who has recently been appointed by the Parliamentary Group as their representative on the Regional Executive Committee.
>
> It was agreed to raise with the Parliamentary Group a suggestion that consultations be arranged in the region between members of the Group and Parliamentary Candidates.
>
> *Annual Meeting 1969*
> Secretary reported that the AEF Hall, Birmingham, had been booked for the 1969 Annual Meeting already arranged for Sunday, 18th May 1969.
>
> *Date of Next Meeting*
> It was agreed the next meeting of the Regional Executive Committee and Sub-Committees be held on Saturday, 22nd February 1969.[5]

A similar range of issues is dealt with by Conservative Party area executive committees, as the following example indicates:

> 1   Chairman's Opening Remarks.

2   To Receive Apologies for Absence.

3   To Approve the Minutes of the Meeting held on 12th February, 1972.

4   To consider Matters Arising.

5   To Receive a Report on the 1972 Quotas.

6   To Recommend the name of one Representative to serve on the National Union Central Council.

7   To Recommend the election of four Representatives to the Executive Committee of the National Union.

8   To Appoint four Representatives to serve on the Area Local Government Advisory Committee.

9   To make recommendations regarding the Election of Honorary Vice-Presidents and Honorary Members.

10   To set up a Sub-Committee to consider Notices of Motion for the Party Conference.

11   To Receive a Report on the 1972 Local Government Elections.

12   To Agree the venue for the 1973 Area Weekend Conference.

13   To Agree the dates and places of future Meetings.

14   To Consider any other business.[6]

Labour Party regional executive sub-committees have not proved very successful and there has been little interest in work at this level. All too often deliberations have tended to be rushed, with insufficient time allowed for each sub-committee. In the West Midlands, for example, the executive committee traditionally meets five times a year and during the 1960s all sub-committees met on the same day. A typical programme was as follows:

Education Sub-Committee	10.00 a.m.
Local Government Sub-Committee	10.30 a.m.
Organisation and Propaganda	11.30 a.m.
Lunch	12.00 noon
Trade Union Sub-Committee	2.00 p.m.
Regional Executive Committee	2.30 p.m.[7]

This system was nonsensical. Able trade union leaders wasted their time enacting a meaningless façade. Instead of formal sub-committees, regional working parties are now established when the need arises. For example, in 1970 the West Midlands region had the following four working parties functioning: (1) a Regional Council Working Party set up in 1968 to study the report of the Royal Commission on Local Government; (2) a Health Service Working Party; (3) an Education Working Party; (4) a Housing Working Party.

126

In the Conservative Party, the level of interest in democratic area organisation varies markedly. Remote constituencies tend not to participate in area activities. In addition, when occupied with local government work, party members often give little time to the area and, when out of local government office, they frequently devote more time to area matters.

There is often competition for places on area council executive committees. In the West Midlands, for example, the position in 1968 and 1969 was as follows:[8]

Table 7.1
Competition for places on the West Midlands Area Council
Executive Committee, 1968, 1969

1968 for	5 men	19	nominations
	5 trade unionists	6	
	5 women	11	
	5 Young Conservatives	8	
1969 for	5 men	16	nominations
	5 trade unionists	4	
	5 women	14	
	5 Young Conservatives	8	

According to one area agent: 'The people who sit on the area executive committee are not dynamic. They do it because they think prestige is involved.'[9] Through the area structure, an ambitious person, such as an aspiring Parliamentary candidate, can meet a large number of influential people. The area executive is often more of a social than a political group, since most work at this level appears to be done, not by the elected element, but by the Central Office area agents who service the committee and its various sub-committees.

In the Labour Party, competition for places on regional council executive committees is not particularly intense. There is occasionally some competition in some of the categories but, equally, there are sections where no nominations are submitted for the available vacancies. In 1970, for example, there were 16 nominations for the 14 available seats in the trade union section on the North-West Regional Council; there were 16 nominations for the 8 vacancies in the constituency parties section. There were, however, no nominations for the one vacancy in the Federation of Trade Councils section.[10] In most other regions there was even less competition for the seats on the regional executive committee.

The majority of resolutions submitted for discussion at a Labour Party regional annual meeting come from constituency parties. Trade union delegates usually come into action only when there is something directly affecting their particular interests. For example, the National Union of Railwaymen was particularly active during the rationalisation of British Rail instituted by Lord Beeching early in the 1960s. The contraction of the mining industry during the same period drew a similar response from the National Union of Mineworkers. There has, however, been a limiting factor on the usefulness of regional annual conferences, namely the ruling that discussion must be limited to regional matters. Until 1971, there could be no discussion of broader national issues. Over the years, this limitation has provoked strong reaction from a variety of quarters. George Brown highlighted many of the grievances at the 1968 Annual Party Conference:

> At every regional conference I go to I am struck by the irrelevance of much that goes on there; I am struck by the sense of frustration which the delegates have who come there . . . I do not see any reason why regional conferences . . . should not spend a good deal of their time talking about these major issues instead of the seemingly endless resolutions that never get anywhere or see the light of day, once they have been nagged about. [11]

The reformers' major concern seems to have been to increase the standing of the Labour Party's regional conferences.

By 1971, the NEC had decided to sail with the wind, and put before the party conference a proposed constitutional amendment lifting the ban on the discussion of national issues at regional conferences. This was accepted and put the Labour Party in line with Conservative practice — although in many respects the distinction is rather academic, since it is the exception, rather than the rule, for any notices of motion to be discussed at Conservative area council annual meetings. Whereas Labour Party regional conferences are more concerned with debate and discussion, Conservative area meetings are essentially formal occasions at which the required business is hurriedly completed before the meeting draws to a close. One could argue that this merely reflects different notions within the two parties concerning discussion: one party encouraging debate, the other discouraging it.

One Conservative area agent asserted that he was 'not at all enthusiastic about area committees. The only useful ones are the Women's Advisory Committee, the Young Conservatives Advisory Committee and, to a lesser extent, the CPC Advisory Committee. The rest of them do not do much, but on the other hand they are not doing much harm, and if they keep talking long enough they might come up with something useful. They are vested interests for people, but the national party structure needs such units at area level, therefore they remain.'[12] Although comments like this may be inevitable, they are nevertheless important. After attending annual meetings and area committees, and after examining documentary evidence at the regional and area level, the author's overriding impression was that the democratic element in both parties was heavily dependent on the professionals who take the bulk of organisational initiatives.

The North-West regional organiser has outlined some of the work involved in co-ordinating the voluntary side of regional organisation:

> . . . A Regional Organiser is Secretary to the Regional Council. In this capacity, particularly in a Region like the North West, he does, in fact, carry out a great deal of work. At the moment, I am engaged in two operations:- (a) I am now attempting to co-ordinate the activities of the Labour members of the new Passenger Transport Authorities (SELNEC and Merseyside). I am also engaged in consultations with the various Labour Groups in an attempt to give the PTA more public backing. (b) Now that the Tory Government has declared itself against development areas, I am collating information and trying to co-ordinate the activities of organisations influenced by the Labour Party in an attempt to try and bring about a change in the attitude of the present Government. If it carried out the proposals already announced, the area of Merseyside would suffer greatly and the future of Barrow and district would be very bleak. [13]

Conservative Party area agents always act as honorary secretary to their area council and area executive committee. They service and co-ordinate both the activities of these committees and the various sub-committees at the area level.

Area agents and regional organisers are also involved in maintaining contacts with Members of Parliament from their area. The 1970 North-West Regional Council Annual Report observed: 'Close contact has been maintained with the Parliamentary Labour Group. The Regional Secretary has attended a number of Group Meetings at the House of Commons. Mr E. Ogden, MP, and Mr T. Price, MP, have served as Parliamentary Group representatives on the Regional Executive Committee.' [14] On several occasions each year, the regional organiser attends group meetings and addresses the group on matters of regional importance. For example, the East Midlands Group of the Labour Party commented on the 1970 Annual Report:

> The Group has maintained regular liaison with the Regional Council through its Regional Organiser, Mr Jim Cattermole, and at a recent meeting Members were fully acquainted with the recommendations of the Regional Executive Committee Working Party on the Redcliffe-Maud proposals for the reorganisation of Local Government. We are also indebted to Mr Michael English, MP, our representative on the Regional Executive Committee for keeping the Group informed of the activities of the Council. [15]

The Lancashire Plot

While initiatives at the regional and area level appear to be taken almost always by the party organisers, there are undoubtedly exceptions to this generalisation. The outbreak of militant activity in the Lancashire and Cheshire area in 1923 is one such instance. This illustrates the way in which the Conservative Party's area organisation can spring into activity when a region's interests seem to be threatened by national party policy. In Lancashire, the area structure provided a channel through which regional discontent with the government could be registered.

After the Conservative Party's defeat in the 1923 election, Alderman Salvidge, a Conservative Party leader in Liverpool, recorded in his diary: 'The election results were appalling everywhere but nowhere worse than in Lancashire ... Interviewed by London papers a few days after the disaster, I said that those who were responsible for this rushed election might just as well have rolled tons of dynamite into Liverpool to uproot the Conservative Party. ...' [16]

Salvidge and Lord Derby proceeded to mobilise the resentment of their local associations against both the protection issue and the timing of the 1923 election. A special meeting of the Lancashire and Cheshire Area Council was called at Manchester on 9 February to discuss the political situation. The attendance, usually about 200–300, was, on this occasion, nearly 1,000. Colonel Jackson, Chairman of the Party Organisation, and Admiral Hall, Principal Agent, came up from London to put the case for Central Office. The chair was taken by Lord Derby who, according to Alderman Salvidge, was 'eager for Lancashire to make its voice heard but anxious that the party managers should not be unduly embarrassed'. For this reason, the press was excluded, but, after the meeting, Lord Derby made an official statement in which he described the proceedings. [17] Colonel Buckley, a Conservative free trader, had tabled a resolution which would have placed on record 'the dissatisfaction [of the meeting] with the policy of the Conservative Party in forcing an election on the issue of Protection', and urging that 'protection should be definitely abandoned as a plank in the policy of the party'. This resolution was seconded by one MP and supported by another. Then Alderman Salvidge tabled an amendment:

> That this meeting . . . believing that the verdict of the country at the recent election was against a change in the fiscal system, respectfully represents to the leaders of the party that it is undesirable that Protection should be included in the programme of the Conservative policy at this juncture. Further, it respectfully protests against the methods adopted previous to the recent General Election when an appeal was made to the electors on the issue of Protection without affording the party organisations throughout the country an opportunity of expressing their opinions thereon; and urges that, with a view to securing in the future greater harmony and better to obtain the representative opinion of the party, a satisfactory method of *liaison* be established between the leaders of the party, the Central Office, and the local organisations. [18]

Colonel Jackson intervened for Central Office and apparently tried to 'head the delegates off from expressing a definite opinion on policy', [19] but his advice was ignored. Salvidge's motion was carried, according to Lord Derby's statement, 'by an overwhelming majority'.

In this instance, the area structure provided a channel through which regional discontent with national party policy could be expressed, although there was 'no thought of disloyalty to the Head Office . . . and the main thought pervading the meeting was to restore the feeling of mutual confidence and to arrive at the best methods of giving expression to the principles for which they stood and from which they had never wavered'. [20] The structure enabled Lancashire to register a firm protest against Baldwin's protectionist policy.

The Conservative Party's area structure has never been used quite so dramatically in subsequent years, but its potential, given dynamic leadership, was demonstrated in 1923. In the more limited life of the Labour Party, there has been no challenge to the party leadership through regional activity. No doubt this is partly because of the long-standing limitation on discussion at the regional level, which was only lifted by the NEC in 1971. There have, of course, been resolutions passed at regional conferences criticising party policy, but these are treated as any other resolutions. In the Labour Party discontent with the leadership is usually expressed through resolutions, but, on an issue of wide regional significance, the possibility of the type of protest engineered by Derby and Salvidge in the North-West cannot be ruled out.

Amateur leadership

In the Conservative Party area chairmen have a very important role to play in party organisation. Their formal role has been outlined in the following way:

1 He is the elected leader of the voluntary organisation of the party.

2 He presides at meetings of the Provincial Area Council and Executive Committee, and endeavours to ensure that their conclusions are representative of the view of the Party as a whole throughout the area.

3 He interprets such views to the Executive Committee of the National Union, and to the Chairman of the Party Organisation whenever opportunities for consultation arise.

4 He should, if possible, be personally acquainted with constituency officers and agents in order to be able to appreciate their problems.

5 He should be available to advise the Central Office on problems concerning the Area as a whole, and to lend his influence where it is required to deal with difficult problems in constituencies.

6 He lends his support and influence to the encouragement of constituency activities in connection with national schemes for the advancement of the Party; e.g. national membership campaigns, speaking competitions, cinema propaganda, schemes for the training of canvassers.

7 He encourages and fosters the development of specialised Party activities within the Area in conjunction with Local Government Elections, political education, Conservative Trade Unionists, Teachers' Associations, etc.

8 He tries to ensure that the recommendations of the Party Headquarters in respect of organisation are put into effect in the constituencies.

9 He advises the Standing Advisory Committee on Parliamentary Candidates when requested in particularly difficult cases.

10 In consultation with the Area Honorary Treasurer he assists the

Area representatives of the Board of Finance in their relationship with constituencies, encourages the raising of the constituency quota for the Central activities of the Party, and keeps the Treasurers of the Party in touch with the Area's financial needs. [21]

The Final Report of the Committee on Party Organisation (1949) recognised that, given the wide range of duties outlined above, the area chairman needed to 'be a man of outstanding energy, distinction and tact'. Proposing a maximum tenure of office of five years, the report asserted: 'He could then hope to make himself familiar with the working of the area and ensure continuity of policy. There may well be fifty to eighty different constituencies in his area, each one of which has its own Conservative Association and Constituency office. He should know personally all the Constituency Chairmen, Treasurers and agents.' The report did, however, recognise that it would be difficult to find 'twelve such men or women – outstanding personalities who are able and willing to devote to the activities of the office of Area Chairman a large proportion of their time'. [22] Attending both constituency association annual meetings and the meetings of the Party Executive Committee and General Purposes Committee in London, dealing with area executive committee matters and chairing the area executive committee meetings are all very time-consuming commitments. This therefore effectively precludes a wage-earner becoming area chairman. Normally the post is filled by leaders in industry and people with sufficient free time to give to such a demanding job.

Professor J. Blondel has examined the background of the forty-three people who held the post of chairman in the twelve areas during the period 1952–62. Of these, twenty-nine appeared in *Who's Who,* 'twelve perhaps because they were MP's, but seventeen on account of their social prestige only'. Blondel observed: 'This never happens for the prospective holders of the office on the Labour side.' [23] In the Conservative Party, 'of the twenty-seven [area chairmen] whose education could be traced, twenty-two had been to public school and twenty had been to universities or equivalent places of higher education, nine had been to Oxbridge and five to one of the Service Colleges. . . . Of the twenty-eight Chairmen whose occupation could be traced, thirteen were in business, in most cases big business; seven had been in the professions, five in the Services and three in the Civil Service or another public body.' [24] The upper middle class nature of the area leadership is unmistakable. The nature of the work, coupled with the social pyramid within the Conservative Party, means that there is no place for the wage-earner in the top ranks of the area structure.

Conservative Party area chairmen are far more than simply figureheads. They are instrumental in providing a channel of information supply to the leadership. They serve to transmit intelligence from the constituency associations to the party leadership and are also frequently used by the leaders to put forward particular policies at the constituency level. In recent years there have been some examples of the way in which area chairmen have become a very important channel of communications within the Conservative Party. When he became Conservative Party Chairman in 1967, Anthony Barber was fully 'sensitive to the criticism that Mr du Cann [his predecessor] had mishandled the area chairmen, [so] he paid careful attention to their views and assiduously passed their constituency reports to Mr Heath, even when they were critical of him. It is indicative of the importance he attached to their role that when he returned to Central Office with Mr Heath on the day after the election he corrected a BBC commentator who announced that they were returning to thank the headquarters staff, insistently adding that they were also coming to thank the area chairmen.'[25] In 1968, following Enoch Powell's famous April speech on immigration, the area chairmen, despite the Powellite sympathies which some of them shared, were used by the leadership to defend Mr Heath at the constituency level.[26] On 7 January 1974, Lord Carrington, the Party Chairman, sounded out the opinions of area chairmen as to the date of the forthcoming General Election. Although three-quarters of his guests favoured an early election, Mr Heath did not go to the country until 28 February.

The above examples indicate that Conservative Party area chairmen are integral parts of the party's communications network. Nevertheless, the seriousness with which area chairmen view their work varies enormously. Goodwill visits to constituency associations are very time-consuming and many area chairmen do not manage to fit many into their programme. This encourages the danger that an area chairman will present a false picture of local party activities to the National Executive Committee or the General Purposes Committee through not having visited more than one or two constituencies. While the party chairman has other means of determining opinion in the country, area chairmen still remain important links between the party in the country and the leadership in Parliament. Their counterparts on the Labour side have no such role to play.

In the Labour Party, regional council chairmen have little importance. Often the position is rotated annually on the basis of seniority. It is purely a sinecure, a reward offered for loyal service at the regional level. A Labour Party chairman tends to be a figure of little importance; a secretary usually assumes the responsibilities and duties which, in the

Conservative Party, are often undertaken by the chairman. One former regional organiser observed that the 'regional council chairman is not important. You use him.' He is frequently called upon to make a statement to the press, but, as this bureaucrat added, 'You never let the chairman go round the constituencies and interfere.' [27] In the Labour Party, the regional chairman is usually an ordinary constituency worker or trade union official (or, occasionally, an MP) who has frequently earned the position by virtue of seniority. His responsibilities appear to be minimal.

The Lancashire Plot illustrates how the area structure could be used for overtly political ends. A similar example occurred in 1972 when Mr Enoch Powell was at the centre of the controversy. In 1972, the West Midlands Area Executive Committee nominated Sir Tatton Brinton as president of the area in succession to Sir Hugh Fraser, who retired after five years in office. Usually presidents are elected unopposed and emerge from behind the scenes. In 1972, however, Powell was also nominated as president for what appeared to be overtly political reasons. According to *The Birmingham Post,* Brinton triumphed over Powell by a 4:3 vote with over 400 constituency representatives attending. [28] As in 1923, the area structure demonstrated its potential to locally based politicians, but this time Enoch Powell was defeated in his apparent desire to undermine the Conservative Party leadership.

Despite the importance of Conservative area chairmen, the permanent officials in both parties remain firmly in control at the regional/area level. While it is true that both the Labour and Conservative Parties retain elaborate democratic structures at the regional level which frequently serve as important channels of communication within the respective parties, it is also true that these consist almost entirely of laymen who are unacquainted with all but the rudimentary detail of party organisation. Organisational initiatives are invariably taken by the professionals in each party.

Notes

[1] I. Gilmour, *The Body Politic,* London 1969. This conclusion should be balanced against that in M. Pinto-Duschinsky, 'Central Office and "Power" in the Conservative Party', *Political Studies,* XX, no. 1, March 1972, pp. 1–16.

[2] In 1971, for example, there were 300 people present at the West Midlands Area annual meeting. This was regarded as a good attendance by

the West Midlands Area Agent (J. Galloway, interview, June 1971).

[3] 1973/4 Annual Report, East Midlands Area Conservative Council.

[4] 1970 North-West Regional Council Annual Report, p. 3.

[5] West Midlands Regional Council, Executive Committee Minutes, 7 December 1968.

[6] West Midlands Area Council, Executive Committee Minutes, 20 May 1972.

[7] West Midlands Regional Council, Executive Committee Minutes, 1968/9.

[8] Taken from nomination papers, West Midlands Area Council, 1968, 1969.

[9] Area agent, interview, 9 December 1969.

[10] 1970 North-West Regional Council Annual Report.

[11] 1968 Labour Party Annual Conference Report, p. 196.

[12] Area agent, interview, 28 May 1970.

[13] P. Carmody, North-West Regional Organiser, letter to the author, 29 October 1970.

[14] 1970 North-West Regional Council Annual Report, p. 9.

[15] 1970 East Midlands Regional Council Annual Report, p. 13.

[16] S. Salvidge, *Salvidge of Liverpool,* London 1934, p. 266.

[17] The excerpts from the report of the meeting which follow are taken from a verbatim account of Lord Derby's statement in *Gleanings and Memoranda,* March 1924, pp. 242–3. See also R.S. Churchill, *Lord Derby, King of Lancashire,* London 1959.

[18] *Gleanings and Memoranda,* March 1924, pp. 242–3.

[19] S. Salvidge, op.cit., p. 266.

[20] R.T. McKenzie, *British Political Parties,* London, 1967, p. 240. (Quote from an interview with Lord Derby in *The Morning Post.*)

[21] *The Party Organisation,* Central Office, London 1964, pp. 19, 20.

[22] *Final Report of the Committee on Party Organisation,* 1949, pp. 22, 23.

[23] J. Blondel, *Voters, Parties and Leaders,* London 1963, p.109.

[24] Ibid., p. 109.

[25] D. Butler and M. Pinto-Duschinsky, *The British General Election of 1970,* London 1971, p. 106.

[26] Ibid., p. 107.

[27] Interview, 27 January 1970.

[28] *The Birmingham Post,* 22 May 1972.

8 Regional/Area Activity During General Elections

Introduction

General Elections are an organisational climax for both regional and area staff. Given the inadequacies of their constituency organisation, election campaigns are particularly demanding for Labour Party regional organisers. The gaps in constituency organisation necessitate greater regional involvement at the constituency level than that required in the Conservative Party, which is organised more professionally. This professionalism helps to account for the different roles played by regional organisers and area agents during General Election campaigns.

A study of regional and area activity during General Elections helps to underline the power relationships existing within the two major British political parties. On the one hand, they act as the field agents of the respective head offices, while, on the other hand, they provide a service to constituency associations in need. This chapter examines the roles of regional organisers and area agents with particular reference to the General Elections of June 1970, February 1974 and October 1974.

Despite differences in emphasis both regional and area staff invariably deal with the following matters during General Election campaigns:

1   The selection of any outstanding Parliamentary candidates and election agents.
2   The allocation of national speakers supplied by the respective head offices, to critical and marginal constituencies.
3   Arrangements for the Prime Minister's and Opposition Leader's tour in accordance with the national strategy.
4   Intelligence work, linking head office with the constituencies.
5   The provision of advice on legal, organisational, and publicity matters to election agents and candidates.
6   Press and television work.
7   The initiation and co-ordination of mutual aid within the region or area.

Despite preparation, there are always last-minute problems for regional staff to tackle. One of these is frequently the selection of candidates. When the 1970 General Election was announced, the East Midlands region still had five constituencies without a prospective Parliamentary candidate. Five selection conferences had to be both organised and attended by regional staff: West Derbyshire on 22 May; Louth on 23 May; Melton on 29 May; Derby North on 30 May; Leicester NW on 31 May. In the two 1974 General Elections there was only one candidate adopted after polling day had been announced but, at the outset of a campaign, candidate selection is an obvious priority.

Similarly, shortage of election agents poses some problems for regional staff. Frequently, people have 'to be dragooned at the last moment to fill these jobs'.[1] David Butler and Michael Pinto-Duschinsky have summarised the position at the outset of the 1970 campaign:

> In most parts of the country Labour had still to recruit amateur agents and there were even candidates to be chosen. Regional organisers were therefore involved in a disproportionate amount of work in setting up the constituency campaigns. Assistant regional organisers had to spend a great deal of the time, especially in the first two weeks of the campaign, giving elementary advice to volunteer agents. They helped them to obtain temporary telephones or premises, to fill in nomination forms, to design election addresses, to understand the technicalities of the law and much more. All agents received daily sheets from the National Agent offering legal and organisational guidance, but the less experienced still required direct help from the regional office.[2]

In 1974, fewer election agents were recruited in the last few weeks before election day partly because the near-certainty of elections in both months enabled regional organisers to prepare with relative thoroughness.

During election campaigns, much of the work connected with the allocation of speakers is dealt with at the regional level. In the North-West in 1951, for example:

> In accordance with usual practice national speakers were allocated to regional office and every effort was made to use the services of the speakers in the constituencies where they would be the greatest assistance to the party.[3]

This is, then, a long-standing function at the regional level. A regional organiser or one of his assistants is detailed to meet all national speakers on entering a region. He has to book hotels, order meals, inform the police and pay certain bills *en route*. The overall programmes are determined nationally; regional organisers are required to attend to details which can be handled most conveniently locally.

An unusual example of the detailed work with which a regional organiser has to be concerned occurred in the 1970 General Election. Robert Mellish, Minister for Housing, was scheduled to appear on television on 2 June, while in the East Midlands region. At lunchtime, the regional organiser asked him if he wanted a clean shirt for the occasion. He did, so the regional organiser had to go out and buy one! In dealing with the arrangements for national tours, however, the relationship between Transport House and regional office is seen in its true perspective. Regional organisers act as the field agents for head office, attending to detail which, if dealt with centrally, would cause bottlenecks at Transport House.

Regional office frequently acts as a link between Head Office and the constituencies. For example, early on the morning of 4 June 1970, each regional organiser was telephoned by Transport House and told to contact all central committee rooms and instruct candidates not to comment on the attack on Powellism made the previous evening by Anthony Wedgwood Benn. (The Prime Minister made a statement later in the day.) On another occasion, there was an urgent directive from the national agent asking regional organisers to instruct candidates to remain inside committee rooms during the Prime Minister's tour as the party was losing television time because, if one candidate was shown, the television network was obliged to provide coverage for his opponent.

There is always a tremendous amount of formal liaison between Transport House and regional organisers during a general election. On 1 June 1970 the party's general secretary asked regional organisers to determine how many constituencies in each region required copies of special election material printed in four languages, Bengali, Urdu, Gujrati and Hindi:

> Head Office will make the leaflet available, free of charge, to any constituency who requires it, and we should be grateful if you would ascertain from the constituencies in your region, how many leaflets they will require, and specify very clearly the quantities for each language that they require.
>
> Will you please take *immediate* action on this matter, as time does not allow us to circulate every constituency, and therefore you will

appreciate that arrangements must be made by telephone with the constituencies in your area to which this is applicable.[4]

Such letters abound during general election campaigns. For example, on 29 May 1970 the national agent sent the following letter to all regional organising staff:

Dear Colleague,
Nomination of Candidates

The most important task now is to ensure that all our candidates are successfully nominated. As you will know the last day for nomination is Monday next 8th June.

Every effort should be made to ensure that all candidates get their nomination papers handed in *this* week so that they may be checked.

I enclose a correct form of Nomination Paper so that you can check any nominations before they are handed in. Please make absolutely certain that our candidates are using this new form.

I would be grateful if you would let me know as soon as each candidate is successfully nominated. . . .[5]

While there is a considerable amount of both formal and informal liaison between Transport House and regional staff, general elections also see a detailed and close relationship between regional organisers and constituency parties. In 1970, the Labour Party had only 141 professional agents at the constituency level; by 1974 this had fallen to 120. Because of the large numbers of voluntary agents manning constituencies, regional staff provide additional formal supervision to the daily guidelines sent out by Transport House. The East Midlands region during the 1970 General Election is used as the major example in this section.

On 18 May, the following letter was sent by regional office to constituency party secretaries:

As you know, polling day in the General Election is Thursday, 18th June and all Cabinet Ministers and Members of Parliament required for meetings will be allocated from this office. I shall be glad, therefore, if you will let me know as soon as possible the dates on which you will require outside speakers. When sending your information, please let us know the name of the hall and the time of the meeting, in order to save time.

We have ample stocks of election material and perhaps you could order your requirements early . . .

Perhaps you would note that as from Tuesday 19th May, the

140

office will be manned from 9 a.m. to 9 p.m. on weekdays and from 9 a.m. to 5 p.m. on Saturdays.[6]

I shall be glad if you will let me know as soon as possible the address of your committee room, the telephone number and the name of the election agent where we do not already have this. Obviously the election campaign is going to be short and sweet, and whilst I appreciate the timing has been totally unexpected, I know I can rely on you to prosecute a most effective campaign. If at any time we can be of assistance to you, please do not hesitate to get in touch with us.

We have divided the region up between the three members of the organising staff and we shall be visiting you for preliminary discussion within the next week.[7]

On 21 May 1970, a further circular was sent out to the constituencies. This indicates the type of detail with which regional office is concerned during a campaign:

We would take this opportunity of bringing to your attention a number of points in connection with the General Election.

1   Committee Rooms
We are still waiting for details of some central committee rooms and telephone numbers. Perhaps you could let us have them as soon as possible as it is holding us up in the preparation of a directory for the region which we want to circulate to all parties as soon as possible.

2   Speakers for Meetings
Requests for speakers should be made to this office, *not* Transport House, and perhaps you could let me have your requests as soon as possible.

3   Office Hours
At the request of Transport House, the office is being kept open until 10 p.m. each evening and 6 p.m. on Saturdays. The office will also be manned during the whole of the Spring Bank Holiday, including Sunday, at least until 6 p.m. in the evening. Transport House will also be open for the same times.

4   Finance
Transport House have already sent out their letter about finance, and if you have not returned your form to us, perhaps you would do this as soon as possible, as Transport House are anxious for their cheques to be issued early in the campaign. We have issued our customary

General Election appeal and we shall be making grants to constituencies at the end of the campaign when parties have a complete picture of the finances of the election. We shall also be sending to some constituency parties receipted invoices for services which have been undertaken by Regional Office and to cover such items as special election appeals which might be issued by other organisations such as the Miners' manifesto, which is certain to be issued to mining constituencies in the region and which is published by the National Union of Mineworkers.

5 Election Material
We have ample supplies of election material, but perhaps you would let us have your orders quickly and we will try and deliver them on our tours of the region.

6 Selection Meetings
Those constituencies re-selecting their sitting Member of Parliament should remember that when completing the financial agreement on the nomination paper the Hastings Agreement[8] was amended last year and advantage should be taken of the increases approved by Conference. If you want details of this perhaps you would contact me.

It is not our intention to circulate you very often, only when it is absolutely essential. Please do not hesitate, however, to get in touch with us if you have any difficulties.[9]

These letters provided certain basic information, particularly useful for voluntary election agents. They also served to reassure the often inexperienced volunteers that regional office was always on hand to help.

In addition to formal liaison with constituency parties, regional staff always provide a very important back-up service in the form of visits – particularly to marginal constituencies. In the February 1974 General Election, for example: 'The [East Midlands] regional staff were allocated to areas in the region, each of which contained marginal seats for special attention. Constant help was given to every constituency throughout the campaign.'[10] The following summary from the log book of an assistant regional organiser provides an indication of the type of work and the difficulties faced by organising staff during the 1970 General Election:

1st June
9.00 a.m. Visit to Labour-held marginal: Attempt to persuade the election agent that he needed the services of a shorthand typist for

the campaign although they had not provided for one in the budget.
2.00 p.m. Visit to Borough Party with two safe Labour seats: A volunteer had been persuaded to act as election agent for both constituencies at the last minute. The ARO spent time checking and filling in legal forms which the election agent found difficult. The ARO also had to place orders for printing the introductory leaflet.
2.45 p.m. Visit to Labour-held marginal: Dispute with the amateur agent who had altered the venue of an appearance by a Cabinet minister the next day without informing the press. The ARO also prepared a candidate's itinerary for the following day.
5.30 p.m. Visit to another Labour-held marginal: There was little to be done in this constituency as the ARO had spent five days in the constituency during the previous week. The ARO also attempted to find accommodation for a visiting supporting speaker.
7.30 p.m. Visit to a third Labour-held marginal: General discussion on organisational matters with the agent.

2nd June
10.00 a.m. Return to first Labour-held marginal: The remainder of the day was spent here. The ARO dissuaded election agent from sending election envelopes to ward parties for filling without checking against the electoral register that they have been properly addressed. ARO reorganises plans for filling and checking envelopes so that it is done at two centres, and can thereby be more easily controlled.

In addition to formal circulars and visits to the constituency parties, regional staff attempt to transfer workers from safe to marginal constituencies and persuade trade unionists to provide help in the most critical seats. On 28 September 1974, for example, the East Midlands regional organiser wrote to all General and Municipal Organisers as follows:

> You will know the address of the Labour Party Committee Room in your area and your help is very welcome. There are, however, a number of seats where a small swing can give us victory. Any assistance you can give in these seats would be doubly useful and I am attaching a list for your information. [11]

On the whole, however, it is very difficult for regional organisers to persuade party workers to move from safe to hopeless constituencies and the success rate in this dimension of their work has been rather low. Referring to the 1970 General Election, David Butler and Michael

Pinto-Duschinsky have calculated that: 'On the Labour side, about half the CLP's in Labour-held marginals received some outside help, but it never amounted to more than 40 per cent of the total canvassed and in three-quarters of them it constituted less than 10 per cent.' [12] Some of the most successful mutual aid in the Labour Party is achieved informally between neighbouring constituencies rather than through the auspices of regional office.

During a General Election campaign, 'telephone work' is very important. The following examples indicate the range of use:

1   Enquiries about exactly who is eligible for postal votes.
2   Enquiries about whether or not supplies of the popular version of the manifesto are available at regional office.
3   Enquiries about the venues of national speakers.
4   Local radio and television networks requesting information and advice.
5   Enquiries about the need to cancel constituency party dinners and so on once the campaign is under way. In order to avoid accusations of 'treating' regional office normally advise in favour of cancellation.
6   Requests for speakers. These need to be dealt with firmly particularly when non-marginal constituencies request front-bench speakers.

Election day detail is a major concern during the last few days of a campaign. There are two priorities: the manning of committee rooms and the provision of tellers at polling stations, particularly in marginal constituencies. In marginal seats, regional staff check that polling stations in the Labour pockets of such constituencies are manned and that party workers are not wasted by manning stations in areas which have not been canvassed. In the last few days, regional staff ask election agents for a list of polling day committee rooms. They also seek to secure final canvass figures from every election agent. These two pieces of information are required by Transport House; regional organisers act as the collecting and collating agency.

Regional organisers frequently apply military terminology to General Election campaigns. Such language is, however, totally inappropriate as there is no centralised chain of command. Regional staff cannot direct constituencies, as is clearly evidenced by their inability to move party workers from safe to marginal constituencies. All that regional organisers can do is to suggest, advise and persuade. The position is not greatly different in the Conservative Party.

144

The Conservative Party

As in the Labour Party, the initial priorities are the selection of prospective Parliamentary candidates and election agents. At the same time area office invariably sends out some documentation to the constituency parties at the outset of the campaign. On 18 September 1974 for example, one area agent sent out the following note:

General Election

During the course of the General Election I shall be sending to Agents as little paper as possible. It will not be my intention to issue Election Briefs from here in addition to memoranda which you will receive from London. To assist in this object, I shall be grateful if you will deal with the following immediately.

1 Complete the enclosed pro forma of details which will be required during the course of the election. Please let me have one copy back by return post.

2 *Intelligence.* Brief, informative telephonic reports from time to time, in the main on:

(a) Policy, its impact and the issues of most interest to the electors.

(b) Effectiveness of our publicity.

(c) Impact of broadcasts and meetings.

(d) General items of interest which have a bearing on the campaign.

(e) Any special item of importance or urgency, scares and mis-statements, will be of value.

3 *Party Literature.* Seven copies of all election addresses (of all candidates) and other locally produced items, e.g. broadsheets, are required here for onward transmission to London. Please make arrangements for the collection of opposition literature well before Polling Day, as they are virtually impossible to obtain after. Also, when forwarding them, make sure that they are packed carefully.

In addition to the above, we are asked from time to time by the press and television for copies of our candidates' election addresses, if you let [my deputy] have twelve copies of your election address, it will save having the enquiry referred to your office.

4 *Area Office.* Enclosed you will find two copies (one for your candidate) of details of the staffing and hours of opening of this office. We are here to assist as much as possible and telephone queries are always welcome provided that they are not on points

145

which have been answered in the notes from London, or are dealt with in the Election Manual or Notes on Current Politics etc.

5   *Election Press Releases.* From time to time we will release statements to local and national papers regarding the general running of the campaign.

We shall supply the Press with details of meetings to be addressed by Shadow Ministers and will issue drafts of speeches if we are supplied with them.

We are not informing them of the individual meetings organised by constituencies, and which are addressed by your Candidate or of meetings addressed by a visiting Back Bench MP or other supporting speaker. Could you, therefore, *please be sure to supply your local newspapers* with details of these meetings, and any speech extracts supplied to you by the speakers concerned.

6   *TV and Radio Companies.* If any of the Broadcasting Companies contact you over covering any meetings in your constituency, would you please let [my deputy] know immediately. Would you also inform us if they or the national press are contacting you for background information.

7   *Cancelled Functions.* All meetings with speakers arranged from this office are cancelled from today's date. We are not sending notification of these cancellations from here but please let it be known that these meetings are off.

8   *Manifesto.* Would you please ensure that your weekly newspapers receive from you immediately a copy of the full version of the Manifesto.

The Conservative Party takes 'intelligence' far more seriously than the Labour Party, partly because of its larger resources but also because its area agents have ample time to engage in this work. In addition to the references to 'intelligence' in the letter quoted above, two further notes were sent out by the same area agent to election agents reminding them of the importance of 'intelligence' material. On 25 September 1974, the area agent wrote: 'Can I draw your attention to paragraph 2 of my memo of the 18th September. It is important that we get, and we can only get it from you, the general feel of the campaign and public reaction to the various Parties. It is sometimes not realised that the way in which the campaign is conducted at National level is, to a large extent, based on the reports from constituencies through Area offices.'[13] In a further letter sent out later, the same area agent wrote: 'Intelligence reports received so far have been of great value. Do please continue with these up to mid-day

146

Wednesday 9th October.'[14] Intelligence work, then, is at the forefront of area activity during General Elections.

The contrast with the Labour Party is marked. It was not until 28 May 1970, some ten days after the announcement of the General Election, that the national agent sent a circular on the subject to regional staff:

> The Organisation and Publicity Planning Group will be meeting early every morning at Transport House, and in order that we can make the best possible use of our joint endeavours, it is very necessary for me to know how the campaign is shaping in your region.
>
> To do this, I should be grateful if you would prepare, each Sunday, a short report giving these details and post it early enough so that I receive it by first post each Monday morning.
>
> In addition, please do not hesitate at any time to let me have your advice, suggestions or criticism of aspects of the campaign in order (a) that we can improve it and (b) that we can assist you on any matter which is peculiar to your region. [15]

This was the thrust of the Labour Party's intelligence network in 1970. The role played by regional organisers was of little significance compared with that of Conservative area agents. There was some improvement during the two 1974 elections when telex machines were installed in each regional office, but these were not used very frequently. In short, regional organisers have little part to play in the Labour Party's intelligence system.

In the Conservative Party, area agents are left to organise their own intelligence networks and, naturally, there is some variation between areas. In general, however, area staff tend to rely on local election agents to provide them with details of how the campaign is progressing. Their task is to provide information for the area agent on the depth of feeling amongst the electorate, perceptions of the national and local campaign, as well as information about opposition tactics within the constituency. It is obviously difficult for an active constituency member to analyse the local situation objectively and the reliability of information reaching area offices from the constituencies must be open to question. Referring to the February 1974 General Election, David Butler and Dennis Kavanagh observe:

> We had an opportunity to witness the accuracy of some of this intelligence on election day in one Conservative area office. The first stories were of high turnouts in Conservative wards and low ones in Labour areas; the previous reports of likely Conservative gains

seemed confirmed and Central Office was informed. The actual results were 'shattering' to the area organiser; the one seat he thought that his party would lose was held, and none of the four Labour-held seats he thought his party would win were gained. [16]

Conservative area agents play an important part in transmitting information from the constituencies to Central Office but it is difficult to decide how valuable this information is to the centre, given the obvious drawbacks in the party's intelligence network.

Transfer of workers, or 'mutual aid', is an important function at area level during General Elections. In the North-West, area aid to 'critical' seats was begun some fifteen months before the 1970 General Election. Area office arranged a series of meetings between constituencies to discuss details. While the initiatives were taken by area office, details about the numbers and reception of workers were left to the constituency associations concerned. In the North-West in 1970, for example, seven constituencies received aid. For example, Macclesfield worked in Cheadle and the Altrincham and Sale constituency was allocated two wards in Stretford during the campaign. In the West Midlands the Stratford-on-Avon constituency was allocated a ward of 1,500 electors in the Rugby constituency, and they dealt with the delivery of literature, canvassing and the manning of committee rooms and polling stations.

David Butler and Michael Pinto-Duschinsky have observed that, in 1970,

> ... at least two-thirds of Conservative associations in Labour-held marginals received 'mutual aid'. In over three-quarters of these constituencies this had been organised through the area office before the campaign; in 10 per cent of them it had been fixed directly with the constituency that was providing the help; and in the remaining 10 per cent, the arrangements were made during the campaign. Slightly over half the CLP's in Labour-held marginals received outside help, arranged in half these constituencies by the regional office before the campaign.' [17]

The greater sophistication of the Conservative Party's mutual aid efforts can hardly be denied. What is more problematical, however, is the success of the schemes which area offices produce, since the constituency level often takes very little notice of the elaborate plans produced at the area level. The North-West area agent observed: 'It is nonsense to see mutual aid in terms of armies of workers running from constituency to constituency. From what I have heard mutual aid is working better than ever before in the North-West region. Preston is receiving enormous help from North and South Fylde. On some nights up to thirty people are going over to Preston to help.'[18] The area cannot command; all it can do is try to persuade party members in safe Conservative seats to help in nearby marginal constituencies. In the final analysis, the success or failure of mutual aid depends on the degree of enthusiasm at the local level.

Conservative area staff have considerable opportunity to specialise during general elections because of the limited amount of work they are required to do at the constituency level. Each area office invariably produces an elaborate press guide. In addition, area staff are usually in close touch with television networks. In February 1974, for example: 'The [East Midlands] Area Office was in constant touch with the Press and Broadcasting Companies.'[19] Such work tends to be beyond the scope of the Labour Party's regional staff because of their extensive constituency party commitments.

Despite a greater degree of professionalism at the constituency level, area agents still fulfil the important role of passing information and advice to constituencies. In early October 1974, one area agent wrote to all election agents as follows:

> You may have received supplies of a so-called poster from an organisation which calls itself the National Association of Ratepayers Action Groups. These posters do not contain a proper imprint and I would advise that they should not be circulated or used in any way. Furthermore, their use would greatly upset genuine Ratepayers Associations.[20]

In a similar vein an area agent wrote as follows to his election agents in September 1974:

> If I were in a constituency I would give serious thought to the use of loud speakers on Polling Day, in that their use could result in increasing the vote of our opponents and losing the advantage of an efficient fetch-up system, but this must obviously be a local decision.[21]

These two examples clearly indicate the advisory position of area staff, even during a general election. They ask constituencies to comply but they cannot in any sense direct local decision-making during a campaign.

There are, then, certain differences in emphasis at the regional level during general elections, but both regional organisers and area agents are involved with essentially the same type of work: selecting candidates and agents, dealing with visits from national speakers and advising constituency associations. One area agent has provided a useful analysis of his work:

(a) to ensure constituencies have both candidates and agents;
(b) to provide an advisory and information service on organisation, election law and policy;
(c) to allocate speakers and plan their programmes to the best advantage;
(d) to see that there is the best possible organisation in the critical seats;
(e) to help the constituencies in every way possible.

I am not a commanding officer. I have no power. You try to get yourself into a position so people come to you for help and advice. [22]

Conclusion

The relatively poor state of Labour Party organisation necessitates detailed intervention by regional organisers on elementary matters such as filling in nomination forms and designing election addresses. While the large number of voluntary agents receive daily notes from Transport House offering legal and organisational advice, many of the less experienced volunteers still require considerable help from regional office, particularly during the first two weeks of a campaign. Labour Party regional organisers are necessarily involved with routine organisational matters at the constituency level. The Conservative Party presents a rather different picture. Its greater professionalism makes work at the constituency level less essential and enables area agents to focus on other issues during a campaign. Conservative area agents devote a disproportionately large amount of time to matters such as intelligence work, mutual aid, policy matters, press and publicity work. Quite how useful this work is cannot easily be assessed but much of it appears to have relatively little pay-off in return for the time and effort put in at area level. While the genuine usefulness of regional organisers during a General Election campaign cannot easily be denied, the value of area agents is open to question.

Notes

[1] J. Cattermole, *The Labour Organiser,* July/August 1970, p. 141.

[2] D. Butler and M. Pinto-Duschinsky, *The British General Election of 1970,* London 1971, pp. 306, 307.

[3] 1952 Lancashire and Cheshire Regional Council Annual Report, p. 9.

[4] Letter from H.R. Nicholas to regional organisers, 1 June 1970.

[5] Letter from Ron Hayward, Labour Party National Agent, to regional organising staff, 29 May 1970.

[6] Here, at the request of Transport House, the hours of opening were later extended. The office was kept open until 10 p.m. each evening and until 6 p.m. on Saturdays. The office was also manned during the whole of the Spring Bank Holiday, including Sunday, until 6 p.m. in the evening.

[7] Letter from East Midlands Regional Organiser to constituency party secretaries, 18 May 1970.

[8] The 1933 Hastings Agreement governed the limits to trade union contributions for sponsored candidates. The 1969 Annual Conference approved an increase from 50 per cent to 60 per cent in the proportion of an agent's salary that a sponsoring union could contribute in borough constituencies, and from 55 per cent to 65 per cent in county constituencies.

[9] Letter from East Midlands Regional Organiser to election agents, 21 May 1970.

[10] 1974 East Midlands Regional Council Annual Report, p. 6.

[11] Letter from East Midlands Regional Organiser to General and Municipal Organisers, September 1974.

[12] D. Butler and M. Pinto-Duschinsky, op.cit., p. 319.

[13] Letter from an area agent to all election agents, 28 September 1974.

[14] Letter from area agent to all election agents, 3 October 1974.

[15] Letter from Ron Hayward, Labour Party National Agent, to regional organisers, NAD/RO.G.E.5, 28 May 1970.

[16] D. Butler and D. Kavanagh, *The British General Election of February 1974,* London 1974, pp. 237, 238.

[17] D. Butler and M. Pinto-Duschinsky, op.cit., p. 319.

[18] A.S. Garner, North-West Area Agent, interview, 13 June 1970.

[19] 1973/4 East Midlands Area Council Annual Report, p. 6.

[20] Letter from an area agent to election agents, 3 October 1974.

[21] Letter from an area agent to election agents, 25 September 1974.

[22] A.S. Garner, North-West Area Agent, interview, 2 September 1970.

9 Conclusion

Most studies of British political parties have stressed the centralised organisation and structure of power in the Labour and Conservative Parties. Almost without exception, their conclusions have been reached without even a cursory look at regional organisation in the two parties. The existence, let alone the significance, of this organisational level has not been fully recognised. This study has analysed the role of regional organisers and area agents within their respective parties, focusing upon their relationships with national, constituency and city party units. The aim has not been to elevate regional and area organisation to an artificially important position, but rather to examine this organisational level with a view to establishing its precise role. In elaborating this hitherto neglected aspect of party organisation, the study has clarified the nature and extent of centralisation in the Labour and Conservative Parties.

It has been shown that both the Conservative and Labour Parties established regional organisations to serve the needs of their respective leaderships. Conservative and Labour Party head offices still retain relatively detailed control over the work of regional and area staff. For their part, however, regional and area organisers exercise little control over constituency party activities. Constituency associations are voluntary units, and consequently there are few sanctions which regional and area staff are able to use against those which ignore their directives. When pressure is applied, regional and area staff frequently fail to achieve their objectives.

Attention was drawn to the differences which exist at the constituency level in the Labour and Conservative Parties. Labour Party regional organisers are endowed with formal authority at the constituency level in their capacity as National Executive Committee representatives, and they fulfil regulatory roles during the selection of prospective Parliamentary candidates and full-time constituency party agents. The establishment of the National Agency Scheme in July 1969 provided regional organisers with a further source of authority at the constituency level.[1]

Conservative Party area agents have traditionally lacked any such formal authority at the constituency level — although there are some indications that change is imminent. From 1974 onwards, it appears that area agents will have a degree of authority at the constituency level that

153

has hitherto been denied them. This development has its roots in suggested changes to the agency service proposed by Lord Carrington, Conservative Party Chairman, in July 1973:

> It is . . . my intention to begin to introduce the central employment of Agents. I recognise that this cannot be done overnight so I have set what I believe is a realistic target over the next year for central employment in what we agree are the priority seats. These are the seats where the next Election will be won or lost, in other words those seats which we think we have the best chance of gaining or which are most at risk from our opponents. There are 131 of these seats and I propose introducing central employment in them in two stages. We will aim to conclude the negotiations in 84 seats by the end of this year so that their Agents will be employed centrally by the Party with effect from 1st January 1974. In the other 47 seats we hope to conclude negotiations during the first part of next year so that central employment will be brought in on 1st August 1974. . . . I have no doubt that our eventual goal should be central employment right across the board. With that end in mind, I am proposing that all trainee agents, on achieving their intermediate certificate, which allows them to take on their first constituency, will automatically become centrally employed agents.[2]

Despite the official line that 'the gradual introduction of central employment will not destroy the autonomy of constituency associations'[3] there seems little doubt that the introduction of this scheme will permit Conservative area agents a degree of authority at the constituency level not unlike that enjoyed by Labour Party regional organisers. Central employment implies a degree of central control which, on a day-to-day basis, invariably means area control. Many area agents believe that central employment will enable them to provide greater direction at the constituency level and, as one area agent put it, allow them to exert 'much larger influence over their activities'.[4] In practice, however, many constituency associations are likely to resist further incursions from area office.

It has been argued in this study that the Conservative Party's greater professionalism in the constituencies has meant that it has less need of an intermediate organisational level than the Labour Party. The Labour Party not only has fewer full-time constituency agents, but it also has far fewer party activists. In 1974, for example, there were only 120 full-time Labour agents in Britain, while individual party membership was about 350,000. Weak constituency organisation has meant that the Labour

154

Party's regional organising staff fulfils an important organising role at the constituency level, and regional organisers are able to provide a degree of expertise which would otherwise be unobtainable. Often, of course, many of the most poorly organised constituencies are politically 'hopeless' and the provision of aid may be questioned on 'productivity' grounds. Regional aid does, however, enable weak constituencies to maintain a political challenge in circumstances where it would otherwise be extremely difficult.

The Conservative Party, with a relatively large (albeit declining) number of full-time constituency agents and party members, is less dependent on area aid at the constituency level. In 1974, besides having between 1¼ and 1½ million members, the party had 375 full-time constituency agents. Almost all critical, marginal and safe constituencies employed a full-time agent and were, therefore, relatively self-sufficient from an organisational standpoint. Area agents were reduced to merely acting as spectators in all but the most hopeless constituencies. In both parties, regional and area influence is greatest in the least politically significant constituencies.

City parties have traditionally posed problems for area agents and regional organisers. Their relatively self-contained and highly centralised organisational structures have enabled them to resist regional and area pressure to abandon their independent identities and conform to Head Office requirements. However, as city parties are now finding it difficult to employ large organising staffs of their own, they have tended to become increasingly reliant on aid from regional or area office. Most large city associations have been forced, for financial reasons, to allow their chief agents to become deputy Central Office area agents — a change which will undoubtedly enhance area influence within the cities. Labour's borough parties have been obliged to accept substantial aid from regional office as their own machines have withered away to almost nothing. In both the Conservative and Labour Parties, however, the deeply rooted traditions of hostility between city parties and area/regional offices are still evident. The influence of regional and area staff is largely determined by the needs, disposition and resources of individual city parties.

It was postulated in the Introduction that regional organisers and area agents act as the field administrative agents of their respective leaderships. This study has indicated the wide variety of ways in which regional and area staff serve their party leaders. It has also been shown that organisers are subject to detailed supervision by the centre — notably through the reporting-in procedures, which are particularly stringent in the Labour Party. One of the major justifications for the maintenance of regional and area organisation is that it serves to keep the centre informed on party activity at the constituency level. Regional organisers and area agents are regarded as essential links in the chain of information, both from the centre to the constituencies and also from the grass-roots to the party leadership. Although afforded some freedom within nationally determined frameworks of action, regional and area organisers nevertheless remain agents of the centre.

While the desire of both party leaderships for some form of field staff in the provinces stimulated the development of area and regional organisation, it is questionable whether the Conservative and Labour Parties still require such extensive regional networks. In opting for this form of organisational machinery, both parties acted contrary to traditional administrative practice in Britain. Only since the Second World War has Whitehall begun to decentralise its workload to the provinces. Traditionally, London-based civil servants either summoned individuals and delegations to visit them, or else they themselves visited the provinces when the need arose. The decentralised pattern of party organisation is, however, now firmly established in Britain, with regional organisers and area agents fulfilling what are frequently regarded by the National Executive Committee and the Conservative Party leadership as essential tasks. The continuance of this network, particularly in the Conservative Party, is, however, questionable on productivity grounds.

The Conservative Party itself has begun to question the relevance of the present area structure. In the October 1973 edition of *Crossbow,* Sara Morrison, Vice Chairman of the Conservative Party, wrote: 'The present areas are too unwieldy to ensure either job satisfaction for the professionals or useful identification of political needs and objectives for everyone else concerned.'[5] This critical theme was taken up a month later by the East Midlands Area Council, which set up a Review Committee to 'look at and consider aspects of the Organisation within the Area, including finance, and to report back to the Area Executive Committee with recommendations as to how and when the Area could help to effect improvements'.[6] The Review Committee presented its report, which contained a rigorous self examination along with some radical proposals for the future, to the area executive committee on 2 November 1974.

The final report observed:

It would seem that in the years since the War not 'in spite of' but more probably 'because of' better communications, the Area has become less effective as a unit. For example, despite easier travel, Area functions and attendances have declined. Cabinet Ministers can be seen frequently on television — why travel 100 miles across the country to hear leading speakers when they can be easily seen and heard on television?

There is more direct contact between constituencies and the Party Headquarters in London.

The overwhelming weight of evidence supports the view that the most effective way in which activities can be organised to help constituencies is at County level.[7]

The Review Committee proposed organisational units based on counties rather than areas, and it proposed a new role for area agents:

We envisage that a County Organisation would undertake many of the functions carried out by the Area Central Office. For example, arranging speaking tour engagements, local radio, press relations, assisting with the Local Government organisation and boundary revisions.

We believe that Areas would then be rationalised into larger regions. Regional Agents would have enhanced status and would be able to devote their time to giving professional advice and guidance in an executive capacity.[8]

There are signs, then, of an increasing awareness of the deficiencies in the Conservative Party's area structure, particularly in the light of the reorganisation of local government in April 1974. Similarly, reform of the party structure in the light of this reorganisation was a major item on the agenda of the Labour Party's Annual Conference in November 1974. The National Executive Committee's document, *Reorganisation of Party Structure,* was given a thorough airing although the party's regional organisation was largely exempt from scrutiny at the conference. In both parties, however, change is inevitable at the regional level. At a mundane level, the vastly improved communications of the last decade have reduced the need for regionally-based staff. London is no longer remote, even to the most distant regions; thus a system of revolving secondment instead of permanent regional staff is a possible alternative organisational strategy. Given the Conservative Party's relatively efficient constituency organisation, some form of revolving secondment from the centre could well be more useful than the maintenance of an elaborate area network which is often under-utilised. During the 1974 General Elections, for example, while Labour Party regional organisers were heavily committed at the constituency level throughout the campaigns, Conservative Party area agents devoted much of their time to intelligence work. There was relatively little need for area staff to involve themselves at the constituency level. In the Conservative Party, if not in the organisationally weaker Labour Party, the maintenance of an extensive area network is an organisational luxury.

Both regional organisers and area agents operate in a political and social vacuum. There appears to be relatively little commitment to the concept of regionalism or provincial government in Britain. The evidence of the Commission on the Constitution, for example, indicated that in no part of Britain did half the people endorse a new system of regional government. The proportion favouring change was much the same in all regions, ranging from Scotland (47 per cent), the South (46 per cent), the North-West (39 per cent), and the South-West (29 per cent).[9] Along with the absence of natural regions, this lack of commitment has meant that British regional politics is somewhat anomalous. Whether the recent changes in local government will strengthen the regional concept by creating larger local authorities is open to question. [10] Similarly, the implementation of at least some of the proposals of the Commission on the Constitution could well strengthen regionalism in Britain. At present, however, regional organisers and area agents are operating in splendid isolation at the regional level.

It has been shown in this study that there is no chain of command from the party leaderships to the constituency and branch levels via regional and area organisers. The chain of command from the centre ends at the regional level. Regional organisers and area agents cannot act as centralising agents for their parties because, although their own relationship with the centre is tightly controlled, they themselves have generally lacked formal authority at the constituency level. The voluntary nature of constituency parties often makes it extremely difficult for regional and area staff to exert influence, let alone authority, at the local level. The importance of regional organisers and area agents within their respective parties must not be exaggerated, although, at the same time, without an acknowledgement of the role of regional and area organisation, our picture of British party organisation is incomplete.

Notes

[1] In 1974 there were 41 agents employed in this scheme.

[2] Conservative Central Office News Service Release, 20 July 1973, p. 2. See also, 'Tory agents will be employed centrally in reformed structure' by John Grosser, *The Times,* 21 July 1973.

[3] Conservative Central Office News Service Release, op.cit., p. 4.

[4] Area agent, interview, 11 October 1973.

[5] Sara Morrison, 'Remaking the Party Machine', *Crossbow*, October 1973, p. 11.

[6] East Midlands Area Council Annual Report, 1973/4, p. 12.

[7] Final Report of the East Midlands Area Review Committee, November 1974, p. 2.

[8] Ibid., p. 6.

[9] *Devolution and Other Aspects of Government*, Commission on the Constitution, Research Paper 7, HMSO.

[10] The 1972 Local Government Act created 39 non-metropolitan county councils and 6 metropolitan counties in England. These new authorities came into being on 1 April 1974.

Bibliography

This bibliography includes only those sources available to the general reader. Some of the original material referred to in this study is contained in the notes, but for a full bibliography of the original sources at both the regional/area and national levels see David J. Wilson, *Regional Organisation in the Conservative and Labour Parties,* Ph.D. thesis, University of Warwick 1974, pp. 293–312. For further reference on wider aspects of party organisation see the excellent bibliography in Richard Rose, *The Problem of Party Government,* London 1974.

Theses

Blewett, N., *The British General Elections of 1910,* D.Phil. thesis, Oxford 1967.

Blondel, J., *The Political Structure of Reading,* B.Litt. thesis, Oxford 1955.

Bochel, J.M., *Activists in the Conservative and Labour Parties – A Study of Ward Secretaries in Manchester,* M.A. thesis, Manchester 1965.

Layton-Henry, Z., *Political Youth Movements in Britain,* Ph.D. thesis, Birmingham 1973.

Pinto-Duschinsky, M., *The Role of Constituency Associations in the Conservative Party,* Ph.D. thesis, Oxford 1972.

Rush, M.D., *The Selections of Parliamentary Candidates in the Conservative and Labour Parties,* Ph.D. thesis, Sheffield 1965.

Urwin, D.W., *Politics and the Development of the Unionist Party in Scotland,* M.A.(Econ.) thesis, Manchester 1963.

Books

Almond, G.A., and Bingham Powell, G., Jnr, *Comparative Politics: A Development Approach,* Boston 1966.

Bealey, F., Blondel, J., and McCann, W.P., *Constituency Politics: A Study of Newcastle-under-Lyme,* London 1965.

Bealey, F., and Pelling, H., *Labour and Politics, 1900–1906,* London 1958.

161

Bealey, F. (ed.), *The Social and Political Thought of the British Labour Party,* London 1970.

Beattie, A., *English Party Politics,* 2 vols, London 1970.

Beer, S.H., *Modern British Politics,* London 1965.

Berry, D., *The Sociology of Grass Roots Politics: A Study of Party Membership,* Macmillan, 1970.

Birch, A.H., *Small Town Politics,* London 1959.

Birch, N., *The Conservative Party,* London 1949.

Blake, R., *The Conservative Party from Peel to Churchill,* London 1970.

Blewett, N., *The Peers, The Parties and The People,* London 1972.

Blondel, J., *Voters, Parties and Leaders,* London 1963.

Buck, P.W., *Amateurs and Professionals in British Politics, 1918–1959,* Chicago 1963.

Budge, I., et al., *Political Stratification and Democracy,* London 1972.

Bulpitt, J.G., *Party Politics in English Local Government,* London 1967.

Butler, D.E., *The British General Election of 1951,* London 1952.

Butler, D.E., *The British General Election of 1955,* London 1955.

Butler, D.E., and Rose, R., *The British General Election of 1959,* London 1960.

Butler, D.E., and King, A., *The British General Election of 1964,* London 1965.

Butler, D.E., and King, A., *The British General Election of 1966,* London 1966.

Butler, D.E., and Pinto-Duschinsky, M., *The British General Election of 1970,* London 1971.

Butler, D.E., and Kavanagh, D., *The British General Election of February 1974,* London 1974.

Butler, D.E., *The Electoral System in Britain since 1918* (Second Edition), London 1963.

Butler, D.E., and Freeman, J., *British Political Facts, 1900–1968,* London 1969.

Butler, D.E., and Stokes, D., *Political Change in Britain,* London 1969.

Chapman, B., *The Prefects and Provincial France,* London 1955.

Churchill, R., *Lord Derby, King of Lancashire,* London 1959.

Clarke, P., *Lancashire and the New Liberalism,* London 1971.

Clements, R.V., *Local Notables and the City Council,* London 1969.

Cole, G.D.H., *British Working Class Politics, 1832–1914,* London 1941.

Comfort, G.O., *Professional Politicians: A Study of British Party Agents,* Washington D.C. 1958.

Cross, J.A., *British Public Administration,* London 1970.

Duverger, M., *Political Parties,* London 1954.

Easton, D., *Varieties of Political Theory*, New Jersey 1966.

Epstein, L.D., *Political Parties in Western Democracies*, London 1967.

Fawcett, A., *Conservative Agent*, National Society of Conservative and Unionist Agents, London 1967.

Feuchtwanger, E., *Disraeli, Democracy and the Tory Party*, London 1968.

Fesler, J.W., *Area and Administration*, Alabama 1949.

Fried, R.C., *The Italian Prefects*, Yale 1963.

Friedrich, C.J., *Man and His Government: An Empirical Theory of Politics*, New York 1963.

Gash, N., *Politics in the Age of Peel*, London 1953.

Gilmour, I., *The Body Politic*, London 1969.

Guttsman, W.L., *The British Political Elite, 1832–1935*, London 1963.

Hanson, A.H., *Planning and the Politicians*, London 1969.

Hanham, H.J., *Elections and Party Management: Politics in the Time of Disraeli and Gladstone*, London 1959.

Harrison, M., *Trade Unions and the Labour Party since 1945*, London 1960.

Hill, R.L., *Toryism and the People 1832–46*, London 1929.

Hindess, B., *The Decline of Working Class Politics*, London 1971.

Holt, R.T., and Turner, J.E., *Political Parties in Action: The Battle of Barons Court*, London 1968.

Holt, R.T., and Turner, J.E., *The Methodology of Comparative Research*, New York 1970.

Hunter, F., *Community Power Structure*, Chapel Hill, North Carolina 1953.

Hurst, M.C., *Joseph Chamberlain and West Midlands Politics, 1886–1895*, The Dugdale Society, Stratford-on-Avon 1962.

Jacob, H., *German Administration since Bismarck*, Yale 1963.

Jackson. R.J., *Rebels and Whips*, London 1968.

James, R.R., *Lord Randolph Churchill*, London 1959.

Janosik, E.G., *Constituency Labour Parties in Britain*, London 1968.

Jones, G.W., *Borough Politics: A Study of the Wolverhampton Borough Council, 1888–1964*, London 1969.

Kavanagh, D.A., *Constituency Electioneering in Britain*, London 1970.

Kavanagh, D.A., *Political Culture*, London 1972.

Kinnear, M., *The British Voter*, New York 1968.

Lasswell, H.D., and Kaplan, A., *Power and Society: A Framework for Political Inquiry*, London 1950.

Leonard, R.L., *Elections in Britain*, London 1968.

Lee, J.M., *Social Leaders and Public Persons*, London 1963.

Leeds, J.D., and Kimber, R., *Political Parties in Modern Britain*, London 1972.

Lowell, A.L., *The Government of England,* 2 vols, London 1908.

McDonald, N.A., *The Study of Political Parties,* New York 1955.

McKenzie, R.T., *British Political Parties* (Second Edition), London 1967.

McKenzie, R.T., and Silver, A., *Angels in Marble: Working Class Conservatives in Urban England,* London 1966.

Mackenzie, W.J.M., *The Study of Political Science Today,* London 1971.

Maddick, H., *Democracy, Decentralisation and Development,* London 1963.

Michels, R., *Political Parties,* London 1911.

Nicholas, H.G., *The British General Election of 1950,* London 1951.

Nordlinger, E.A., *The Working Class Tories,* London 1967.

Ostrogorski, M., *Democracy and the Organisation of Political Parties,* 2 vols, London 1902.

Parry, G., *Political Elites,* London 1970.

Parry, G. (ed.), *Participation in Politics,* Manchester 1972.

Paterson, P., *The Selectorate,* London 1967.

Pelling, H., *Social Geography and British Elections, 1885–1910,* London 1967.

Pelling, H., *The Origins of the Labour Party,* London 1965.

Pulzer, P.G.J., *Political Representation and Elections in Britain,* London 1967.

Rokkan, S., and Lipset, S.M., *Party Systems and Voter Alignments: Cross National Perspectives,* New York and London 1967.

Ranney, A., *Pathways to Parliament,* London 1965.

Rose, R., *Influencing Voters: A Study of Campaign Rationality?,* London 1965.

Rose, R., *The Problem of Party Government,* London 1974.

Rush, M., *The Selection of Parliamentary Candidates,* London 1969.

Salvidge, S., *Salvidge of Liverpool,* London 1934.

Self, P., *Administrative Theories and Politics,* London 1972.

Sharpe, L.J. (ed.), *Voting in Cities; the 1964 Borough Elections,* London 1967.

Simon, H.A., *Models of Man,* New York 1957.

Smith, B.C., *Regionalism in England: Regional Institutions – A Guide,* Acton Society Trust, London 1965.

Smith, B.C., *Regionalism in England 2: Its Nature and Purpose 1905–1965,* London 1965.

Smith, B.C., *Regionalism 3: The New Regional Machinery,* London 1965.

Smith, B.C., *Field Administration,* London 1967.

Toqueville, A. de, *Democracy in America* (Mentor Edition), New York 1956.

Vincent, J.R., *The Formation of the British Liberal Party,* London 1966.

Weber, M., *The Theory of Social and Economic Organisation,* London 1922.

White, R.J., *The Conservative Tradition,* London 1964.

Williams, J.E., *The Derbyshire Miners,* London 1962.

Winnifrith, Sir J., *The Ministry of Agriculture, Fisheries and Food,* London 1962.

Woolton, Earl of, *The Memoirs of the Rt. Hon. The Earl of Woolton,* London 1959.

Young, G.M., *Stanley Baldwin,* London 1952.

Articles

Bachrach, P., and Baratz, M.S., 'Two Faces of Power', *American Political Science Review,* 1962.

Baxter, R., 'The Working Class and Labour Politics', *Political Studies,* 1972.

Beer, S.H., 'The Conservative Party of Great Britain', *Journal of Politics,* 1962.

Bierstedt, R., 'The Problem of Authority' in Berger, M., et al. (eds), *Freedom and Control in Modern Society,* New York 1954.

Birch, A.H., 'A Note on Devolution', *Political Studies,* 1956.

Block, G.D.M., 'On the State of Conservative Studies', *Swinton Journal,* 1968/9.

Blondel, J., 'The Conservative Association and the Labour Party in Reading', *Political Studies,* 1968.

Bochel, J.M., and Denver, D.T., 'The Impact of the Campaign on the Results of Local Government Elections', *British Journal of Political Science,* 1972.

Bochel, J.M., and Denver, D.T., 'Canvassing, Turnout and Party Support', *British Journal of Political Science,* 1971.

Bulpitt, J.G., 'Participation and Local Government: Territorial Democracy', in Parry, G., (ed.), *Participation in Politics,* Manchester 1972, pp. 281–302.

Clarke, M.G., 'National Organisation and the Constituency Association in the Conservative Party: The Case of the Huddersfield Party' *Political Studies,* 1969.

Cornford, J., 'The Adoption of Mass Organisation by the British Conservative Party' in Allardt, E., and Littunen, Y., *Cleavages, Ideologies and Party Systems,* Helsinki 1964.

Cornford, J., 'The Transformation of Conservatism in the Late Nineteenth Century', *Victorian Studies,* 1963.

Cross, J.A., 'The Regional Decentralisation of English Government Departments', *Public Administration,* 1970.

Fesler, J.W., 'Centralisation and De-centralisation', *International Encyclopaedia of the Social Sciences,* pp. 370–7.

Fesler, J.W., 'The Political Role of Field Administration' in Heady, F., and Stokes, S.L., *Papers in Comparative Public Administration,* New York 1962.

Fesler, J.W., 'Field Organisation' in Marx, F.M., *Elements of Public Administration,* New Jersey 1959.

Fesler, J.W., 'Approaches to the Understanding of Decentralisation', *Journal of Politics,* 1965.

Glickman, H., 'The Toriness of English Conservatism', *Journal of British Studies,* 1961.

Hands, G., 'Roberto Michels and the Study of Political Parties', *British Journal of Political Science,* 1971.

Hanson, A.H., 'De-centralisation', *Planning and the Politicians,* London 1969.

Harris, J.S., 'Regional Decentralisation of Government Departments in Britain', *Canadian Journal of Economic and Political Science,* 1958.

Jones, R.B., 'Balfour's Reform of Party Organisation', *Bulletin of the Institute of Historical Research,* 1965.

Lambert, R., 'Central and Local Relations in Mid-Victorian England', *Victorian Studies,* 1962.

McKenzie, R.T., 'Power in British Political Parties', *British Journal of Political Sociology,* 1955.

McKenzie, R.T., 'The Wilson Report and the Future of the Labour Party Organization', *Political Studies,* 1956.

Mackenzie, W.J.M., 'Mr. McKenzie on British Political Parties', *Political Studies,* 1955.

March, J.G., 'The Power of Power' in Easton, D., *Varieties of Political Theory,* New Jersey 1966.

Medding, P.Y., 'A Framework for the Analysis of Power in Political Parties', *Political Studies,* 1970.

Michels, R., 'Authority', *Encyclopaedia of the Social Sciences,* New York 1930.

Morrison, S., 'Remaking the Party Machine', *Crossbow,* October 1973.

Parkinson, M., 'Central–Local Relations in British Parties: A Local View', *Political Studies,* 1971.

Pimlott, B., 'Local Party Organisation, Turnout and Marginality', *British*

Journal of Political Science, 1973.

Pimlott, B., 'Does Local Party Organisation Matter?', *British Journal of Political Science,* 1972.

Pinto-Duschinsky, M., 'Central Office and Power in the Conservative Party', *Political Studies,* 1972.

Robbins, J.H.R., 'The Conservative Intervention in Doncaster Borough Politics', *British Journal of Political Science,* 1972.

Taylor, A.H., 'The Effects of Party Organisation', *Political Studies,* 1972.

Taylor, A.H., 'The Spread of Labour Party Candidature for Parliamentary Elections in the East Midlands and South Yorkshire', *East Midland Geographer,* 1973.

Taylor, A.H., 'Measuring Movements of Electors Using Election Returns', *Political Studies,* 1974.

Trethowan, I., 'The Tory Strategists', *New Society,* 21 May 1964.

Urwin, D., 'Scottish Conservatism: A Party Organisation in Transition', *Political Studies,* 1966.

Wilson, D.J., 'Campaigns and Communications', *New Society,* 1 April 1971.

Wilson, D.J., 'Local Elections', *New Society,* 23 May 1972.

Wilson, D.J., 'Party Bureaucracy in Britain: Regional and Area Organisation', *British Journal of Political Science,* 1972.

Wilson, D.J., 'Constituency Party Autonomy and Central Control', *Political Studies,* 1973.

Index

The Author

Dr David J. Wilson is Senior Lecturer in Politics at Leicester Polytechnic. He received his B.A. and Ph.D. from the University of Warwick, and his B.Phil. from the University of Liverpool. His research interests are local and regional politics and administration, and he has written a number of articles in this area.